Sept 8/

Dec 3/8

	Date D...

1457 PERTH AVENUE
LONDON, ONTARIO
N5V 2M4
(519) 455-5066

*British Columbia: One Hundred Years of
Geographical Change*

British Columbia:

One Hundred Years of Geographical Change

J. Lewis Robinson
&
Walter G.
Hardwick

Talonbooks
201 1019 East Cordova
Vancouver
British Columbia V6A 1M8
Canada

This book was typeset by Beverly Matsu,
designed by David Robinson and printed by
Hemlock Printers for Talonbooks.

Cartography by Karen Ewing.

Fourth printing: May 1979

Canadian Cataloguing in Publication Data

Robinson, John Lewis, 1918-
    British Columbia, one hundred years of
geographical change

    ISBN 0-88922-048-4 pa.

    1. British Columbia - Economic conditions.
I. Hardwick, Walter G., 1932-   II. Title
HC117.B8R6   330.9′711′03   C74-5647-6

Contents

Introduction

During the past century the geographical patterns within British Columbia have changed. Although the natural environment of mountains, rivers, vegetation, soils and climate in the province can be described with superlatives and seems so stable, man's perception of this environment is changing; his adjustments to it are many and different as population increases. In addition, the man-made environment in which most of us live has expanded dramatically as our cities spread over the natural landscape. Just as distribution patterns described in the past are now different, so one can expect that the geography of to-day will differ to some degree in the future. Thus British Columbia has not one but several geographies, each analysing conditions of a particular period of time. These changing geographical patterns of man living in his British Columbia environment is the theme of this book.

The present geography of British Columbia illustrates many physical and human contrasts. The physical landscape has great variety and its scale is impressive. The coast of British Columbia has striking landform variety in its numerous rugged offshore islands, protected alongshore channels, linear fiords twisting inland among jagged coastal mountains, narrow coastal lowlands, low marine terraces and the broad delta of the Fraser River. These coastal features, in turn, contrast with the level horizons of the broad interior plateaus with their deep canyons. The narrow river terraces of the interior valleys are constant reminders of how little level land there is at low elevations.

Variety in the provincial landscapes is intensified by the contrasts in vegetation. Extensive stands of tall, green conifers clothe the lower slopes of the coastal mountains and the west-facing slopes of the interior mountain ranges; smaller trees spread endlessly across the central plateau. In the lee of the mountains, however, and in the dry southern interior valleys, tawny bunch grass and even cactus indicate how sparse the vegetation cover is. In winter the green of trees, grass and shrubs of the mild and wet coast contrasts with blue skies, cool temperatures and snow-covered landscapes of the interior. Man's impact upon the natural vegetation in terms of agricultural clearing and forest logging has modified only a small part of the total natural landscape of the province, but in local areas these patterns of utilization constitute significant geographical changes.

The human patterns of occupance illustrate contrasts in intensity of use. Population is concentrated into the southwestern corner of the province, in urban centres dispersed around Georgia Strait. In 1971 about 75 percent of the population of 2,300,000 resided in this region under conditions of intense use. In the valleys of the southern interior, and northward along the coast, most residents occupy small settlements whose locations reflect either the utilization of local resources or are service centres along transportation routes. Economic activities have dispersed patterns of distribution outside of the southwest corner; they developed in local regions in response to expanding external markets for their desired resources. Most of the northern valleys are almost empty, and throughout the province most of the mountain and upland areas are completely lacking in permanent residents. Few people live on farms, but in terms of area large sections of the south-central interior are used for grazing. Elsewhere in the southern two-thirds of the province extensive tracts of forest are being utilized under tree-farm management or with controlled cutting that should maintain a continuous harvest. However, the number of primary workers in the farms, forests, mines and fisheries is small compared with the number of people employed in the wide range of occupations in the large urban centres. British Columbia is, therefore, a land of contrasts with little uniformity over large areas in either the physical landscape or in man's occupation and use of the land and its resources.

The exploitation of Nature's endowment came gradually, and to different places at different times. The spotty and discontinuous settlement pattern that evolved was a definite contrast to the broad, westward-moving frontier which subdued the Western Plains. A hundred years ago small, sea-oriented settlements were being established in the southwestern corner of British Columbia by people of European origin, but at the same time older dispersed settlements of the interior persisted as remnants of the land-based fur trade or mines. To understand the present geography of British Columbia one must appreciate the increasing functional connections which have tied the urban areas of the coast with the small centres of the interior, and the province as a whole with the rest of North America, Europe and the Pacific countries.

Changing Geographical Position

For 150 years British Columbia has been peripheral to major continental centres of population and commerce; as a result it has been only gradually drawn into the main stream of industry and ideas of the western world. Exploration was only beginning at a time when eastern Anglo-America already had thriving towns and expanding agricultural settlement. The first reports of the natural environment of British Columbia came after Alexander Mackenzie made his way westward to the Pacific in 1793, and Captain George Vancouver simultaneously explored and charted the coast for Britain. This western part of North America was by no means empty when first seen by Europeans. Sedentary native Indian communities had developed a high culture on the coast as they wrested a successful livelihood from the environment as they knew it then.

For several decades after European "discovery" the region remained isolated, being several months by land or sea from Europe. It became one of several "outposts of empire"; its one-product economy was organized around a minor fur trade. Political, economic, and military decisions made abroad, often with little apparent relevance to British Northwest America, influenced the settlement and economy in this region. It was bargained over by the British, American, Spanish, and Russian governments at one time or another, more because of its geographical position than for its potential wealth of resources. The region was like a capped oil well, a capital asset whose riches were only partly known and remained to be exploited. External events gradually changed the relative location of the colony; it became more closely linked to Mother Britain, with other outposts of British commercial enterprise in the Pacific, with nearby California, and finally, nearly a hundred years after discovery, by rail with the eastern coreland of the new Canadian nation. As time passed, the natural resources of fur, fish, forests, and mines became better known; they were exploited when competing resources elsewhere near the major markets of the world were partly depleted.

The changing geographical position of British Columbia with relation to world centres in the 19th century was experienced with varying intensity in different parts of the mountain region. Early in the 19th century European settlement had been initiated by the fur trade in the central interior, known then as New Caledonia. The furs moved eastward across Canada along river transport lines. The scanty fur resources of central British Columbia were being exploited first at about the same time that fur trading posts were being opened down the Mackenzie River valley. Thus to fur trade managers in Eastern Canada the posts of central British Columbia were as remote as those of the Mackenzie Valley in the far northwest. In the western mountains the fur trade, with its dispersed but linked settlements, gradually spread southward to the Columbia River and out to the Pacific coast at Fort Vancouver; from there furs were exported by sea. In 1827, with the building of the fur trading post at Fort Langley, on the Fraser River near its mouth, and with the establishment of Fort Victoria in 1843 to protect British interest on Vancouver Island, a Pacific orientation was given to the fur trade in the colony. As the years passed, the "Pacific door" opened more frequently for the region and communication through the "back door" to the colonies in the East gradually deteriorated. In both cases, however, the lines of transport to fur markets were long and tenuous.

The gold rush of 1858-62 to the central Fraser River and the western flanks of the Cariboo Mountains brought the first large settlements to the interior, and at the same time helped to broaden the commercial functions of centres on the southwest coast. In the 1860s and 1870s the expansion of forestry for overseas trade, as a result of increased demand for forest products in the Pacific basin, brought new activities to the Georgia Strait region. When British Columbia became a province in the new Dominion of Canada in 1871 its seaborne links with the world were firmly established through the southwestern corner. Although British Columbia was first settled from the interior, the coastal region forged ahead and turned its back on the continent. By the turn of the century the southwest corner of the province had become the focus of manufacturing, administration and trade in the western Cordillera. On a local scale within this early heartland around Georgia Strait, there were several decades of rivalry between Victoria and Vancouver for dominance in government, transportation, economic activities and social importance. Their changing fortunes in this competition were in large part related to their changing geographic position. Victoria led as long as the region was served exclusively by ship; Vancouver rose to dominance following the completion of the trans-Canada railroad.

The early settlement of British Columbia had an irregular pace of growth with little coordinated, integrated development between 1871 and 1940. Outside of the southwest new towns were established which saw their success or failure in terms of the local forest, mine or fishing industries upon which each depended. In contrast, the record of the past two decades in all regions is one of increasing division of labour between the communities throughout the province and resulting interdependence. A functional unity has emerged in British Columbia which was almost lacking 100 years ago. Isolated centres have become part of a network of places within recognized provincial regions; the regions, in turn, were gradually linked together, particularly throughout the southern half of the province. The communities of British Columbia moved from isolation to functional integration. And through all this century of change the places around Georgia Strait formed the "heartland" of the province, dominating activities throughout the region. In the next decade of the 1970s the integration of the northern one-third of the province is underway.

Isolation to Integration

The forces which affected the changing geography of British Columbia have not been uniform in time or space. Four periods are suggested in which the pace of change accelerated and the consequent geography of the region was greatly modified: (1) In the period of early European settlement, 1843-1886, two core regions were established— that on both sides of Georgia Strait and the mining frontier in the Cariboo. Although British Columbia became part of Confederation in 1871 it was not effectively linked with Eastern Canada until 1886. (2) The period of post-Confederation speculation, 1886-1918, followed the arrival of the Canadian Pacific Railway. During this time urbanization of the Georgia Strait region increased, and the frontiers of resource exploitation spread northward along the coast and into the southern interior and the southeast. (3) During the period of production expansion, 1919-1946, the coastal economy grew, based on forestry and international trade, and Vancouver consolidated its position of dominance. Resource utilization in the interior was relatively minor and confined to small local areas. (4) The post-war period, 1947-71, has been one of functional integration of the economy and the linking of the various sub-regions of the province. With this integration now well achieved future historical geographers may be able to identify a fifth period of geographical change in the 1970s when the interior and north became more significant in provincial spatial interaction.

These historical events have taken place in particular spatial patterns which are generally concentric zones outward from the core region of Georgia Strait. (Map No. 1, p. 14) In general, the intensity and complexity of economic activity, and the density of population, decrease outward. The central core, the Georgia Strait region in the southwest, is the primate urban, industrial, commercial and trade region of western Canada. The second zone includes the valleys of the southern interior where agriculture and some mining, aided by early railways, supported groups of settlements early in this century. The third zone is a discontinuous semicircle including the Kootenays in the southeast, the central interior around Prince George, and Prince Rupert on the north coast. Urban centres grew slowly in these sub-regions after World War I, based on local resource developments but related to transportation lines. Between the groups of settlements in zone three were large empty areas or thin lines of sparse settlement. The fourth, and outer, zone is occupied by most of northern British Columbia. Settlements are few in this zone, except for the cluster of urban places and extensive farmland in the Peace River area; large-scale resource utilization is just beginning to penetrate into it. As these resource developments are linked functionally with service and supply centres in zone three one may expect the southern part of zone four to gradually merge into zone three.

DEVELOPMENT ZONES OF BRITISH COLUMBIA

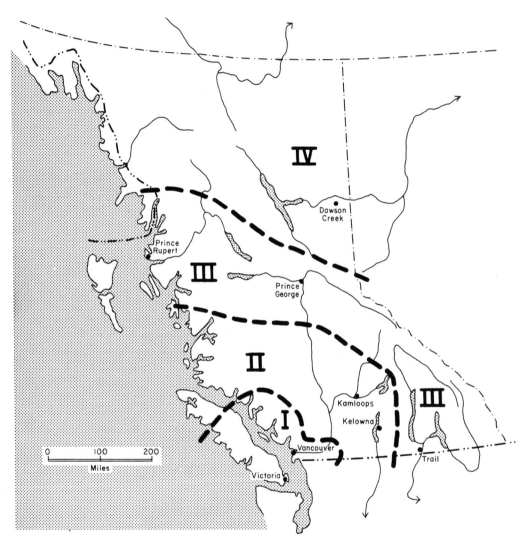

Map No. 1

14

Early Settlement: 1843~1886

Although the whole west coast was occupied for at least five thousand years (possibly about 9000 years) by native Indians with one of the advanced cultures of North America, the occupation by Europeans covers a time span of less than 200 years. Political administration was gradually transferred to a colonial government after the founding of Victoria in 1843 and the establishment of the 49th parallel as the boundary with the United States. Economic utilization of commodities other than furs, excluding minor local use of coal and forests, had to await a major event to draw attention to the region. This event was the discovery of gold in the Fraser River in 1858. Many failed to make their fortunes with gold but stayed to develop a local forest, mining and agricultural economy— all without a transcontinental railroad. It is sometimes forgotten that overseas cargoes were flowing in and out of British Columbia for three decades preceding the founding of Vancouver or the arrival of the Canadian Pacific Railway

to the west coast.

Victoria was the only urban settlement during this early period; Vancouver did not exist. The site for Victoria was chosen by Hudson's Bay Company officials in 1843 to establish a base on British territory on Vancouver Island at the time of the Oregon Treaty. A decade after its founding the relative unimportance of Victoria in western North America is suggested by the following figures: the fort and surrounding cluster of buildings totalled 79 dwellings and 12 stores; the white population of southeastern Vancouver Island was reported as less than 600 persons, of whom about 240 lived in or near the fort, and 140 lived on three large nearby farms which had a total of 350 improved acres; about 700 Indians occupied a village on the west side of Victoria harbour across from the fort. Only 2,000 to 3,000 pelts were receive annually from the fur trade and these declining returns indicated the low state of economic activity in the region. Victoria's origins were indeed humble. The discovery of gold along the Fraser River attracted a few thousand miners to the region and Victoria became a transportation gateway and commercial supply centre for the Cariboo gold fields of the interior. Similar to the function of San Francisco previously, where imported goods were trans-shipped eastward from that city up the Sacramento River to the gold diggings, Victoria became a trans-shipment centre for supplies destined for the interior gold towns of British Columbia.

Victoria was incorporated as a city in 1862, after the boom population of 1858-59 had dwindled away and the city had a more stable population of more than 2,000 persons. By this time most of the original fort buildings had been removed and a small commercial core of one-storey wooden buildings was established, bounded by Johnson, Douglas and Fort streets and the harbour. (Map No. 2, p. 16) A line of wholesalers along Wharf Street indicated the important trans-shipment function of Victoria; a large number of hotels and saloons in the commercial core also told of the city's transit functions. The residential area of the city had spread outward to Rock

VICTORIA LAND USE, 1863

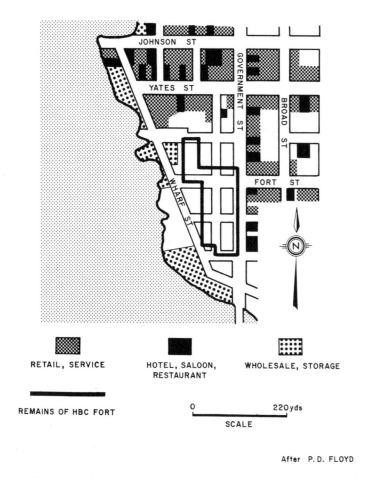

JOHNSON ST

YATES ST

GOVERNMENT ST

BROAD ST

FORT ST.

WHARF ST

RETAIL, SERVICE

HOTEL, SALOON, RESTAURANT

WHOLESALE, STORAGE

REMAINS OF HBC FORT

0   220yds
SCALE

After P. D. FLOYD

Map No. 2

VICTORIA LAND USE, 1890

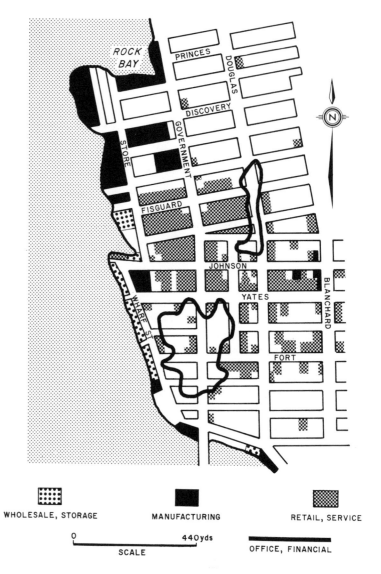

ROCK BAY

PRINCES

DOUGLAS

DISCOVERY

GOVERNMENT

STORE

FISGUARD

JOHNSON

YATES

BLANCHARD

FORT

WHARF ST

WHOLESALE, STORAGE

MANUFACTURING

RETAIL, SERVICE

OFFICE, FINANCIAL

0   440yds
SCALE

Bay on the north, Cook Street to the east, and James Bay to the south (the latter was filled in later and occupied by the Empress Hotel). The government buildings, erected south of James Bay outside of the settlement, were reached then by a small bridge. Outside of the tiny city about 200 persons lived on farms in Saanich and possibly 200 persons were in the village of Esquimalt. The functions of Victoria were almost entirely commercial and administrative. Half of the total of four million dollars of imports in 1863 came from San Francisco, and gold constituted most of the three million dollars of exports that passed through the port.

Victoria's strategic position aided its growth. Its location on Juan de Fuca Strait made it the gateway for entry from abroad. Ships from Britain came slowly, sailing around Cape Horn, and emphasizing the long lines of communication to and from the tiny colony. Victoria was linked by ship southward to American railheads leading to eastern Anglo-America from San Francisco and later from the Columbia River. Victoria's commercial links were strong with California and were almost non-existent with eastern Canada.

When British Columbia joined Confederation in 1871 more than one-third (about 4,400) of the colony's 11,000 to 12,000 white residents lived in or near Victoria. It was the political, economic and social capital of the new province. This pre-Confederation dominance of Victoria gave an initial advantage which permitted it to compete strongly with the mainland centre at Vancouver later in the century.

New Westminster was established in 1858 as the chief commercial and administrative centre for the mainland colony of British Columbia. Its site was selected on the steep north bank of the Fraser River, a short distance upstream of the delta mouth. The position of the settlement, overlooking the section where the several channels of the Fraser River entrance became one river, gave control over river traffic. However, in contrast to easy access to the good harbour at Victoria, approaching New Westminster was difficult for sailing ships with cargoes from abroad because of relatively shallow river depths, and the shifting channels. The political and commercial rivalry between Victoria and New Westminster for dominance, both within the southwest region and over the interior, was partially settled in 1868 when Victoria was named the capital of the union of the two colonies.

Another of the early urban centres of the Georgia Strait region, Nanaimo, was settled in the 1850s as a resource-based port. Coal seams exposed there could be mined from shallow shafts. The coal was first exported to Victoria for space-heating purposes, but a major market was developed soon in San Francisco. Later, as the only tidewater coal field on the North American west coast, Nanaimo and other nearby coal fields became important for bunkering purposes. This movement of coal was another example of the north-south ties which were strengthening along the Pacific Coast. Nanaimo, and the Burrard Inlet sawmill settlements, were examples of the resource-based towns which were to arise elsewhere in British Columbia in the next 100 years. Their local economy then, even as now to a lesser degree, depended on external conditions and markets elsewhere in the world.

Lumbering activities had become established on the south coast prior to 1871. The coniferous forests were extensive and the huge size of the trees threw despair into the minds of prospective farmer-settlers. Cutting down the large trees was difficult enough but the removal of stumps was a formidable task. The big trees of the local physical environment had little value within the region; their utilization depended upon finding markets elsewhere. The impetus for commercial cutting was created by external British domestic and naval needs believed threatened by the American Civil War. Lumber mills were erected at Alberni and at Burrard Inlet in the early 1860s but little lumber and only a few spars ever went to Britain. An export market was obtained by supplying expanding British commerce in several Pacific ports. California did not become an immediate market for lumber because of the intervening sawmills already producing in Puget Sound and in Oregon.

The two mills established in 1863-65 on the opposite sides of Burrard Inlet provided a focus for the British Pacific lumber trade. The mills were small but self-sufficient in terms of using nearby timber. Harvesting was limited to accessible coastal strips near tidewater until the technology and equipment of that time could be adapted to the problems of harvesting large trees. Two small settlements grew up around these sawmills, supplying housing, food, drink and services to the workers at the mills. On the north shore Moodyville was to grow into North Vancouver, and on the south side Granville was to become Vancouver. When British Columbia became part of Canada in 1871, the townsite of Granville was being laid out and the province's largest city, Vancouver, was establishing its humble beginnings. To the local residents then Granville was sometimes called "Gastown" because of talkative "Gassy Jack" Deighton, a saloon and hotel keeper of the late 1860s. (This name was revived in the 1960s for the restored old part of the city.)

Farms were established during this period both on the coast and in the interior. The occupation of land for farming was part of the general movement which had brought people west to Oregon Territory twenty years earlier, but preemption regulations and costs of land were not as attractive in the Fraser Valley as in the adjoining American states. Land clearing was slow if lumbering had not preceded, but on southern Vancouver Island some farms could be established on natural grassland clearings. On the floodplain delta of the Fraser River drainage was a problem and in addition crude dykes had to be constructed to lessen the danger from annual floods. Some of the larger farms were cleared at the eastern end of the Fraser Valley, near present-day Chilliwack, because they were close to the market for food in the Cariboo goldfields.

Although the Cariboo Gold Rush had prompted much of the commercial expansion in Victoria and New Westminster on the southwest coast, its prime function was to extract gold, and this activity resulted in the first large settlements in the interior. In the early 1860s Barkerville and the nearby Cariboo goldfields had the largest concentration of people in western Canada. The engineering feat of building the Cariboo Road through the Fraser River canyon was accomplished, linking the resource-based economy of the goldfields with the coastal administrative and commercial centres. (Map No.3, p. 19) Cattle ranches and farms were established on the interior grasslands to help feed the miners and their communities. Cattle had been driven north along the intermontane valleys of the American Cordillera, and some reached the Chilcotin grasslands at least a decade before ranching was established in Montana. However, by the time that Confederation was being discussed in eastern Canada the bloom of the Cariboo Gold Rush was about over. Some people stayed in the central interior, settling on small farms or large ranches in the Chilcotin, Fraser and Thompson valleys. When traffic and population declined in the goldfields the flow of a few agricultural products, particularly beef, reversed; some sparse markets were found in the few small towns on the coast.

Some of the nodes of future larger settlements in the interior remained. Along the Cariboo Road clusters of buildings at Lillooet, Ashcroft, Clinton and 100 Mile House had arisen as resting places and minor collecting centres, but no real service towns emerged. (Map No. 3, p. 19) The Cariboo Road, like the Dewdney Trail to the Kootenays later, was a transport link to the coast which had renewed significance several decades later. Following the decline of mining in the interior, economic activities in British Columbia remained essentially coastal during the 1870s.

The European settlement of the northern part of the interior was long delayed. The flurry of the Cassiar Mountains gold rush had no permanent impact on the landscape. As a result of an external decision the Bulkley Valley in the northwest was entered in 1866 when it was selected as part of the route of a proposed telegraph line to link the United States with Europe via Alaska and Siberia. But another external decision

THE CARIBOO ROAD TO THE GOLDFIELDS

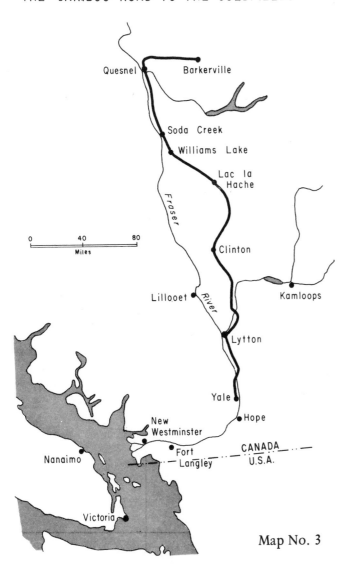

Map No. 3

and the resultant Atlantic Ocean cable removed the surveyors from this little-known region. For several decades to follow much of northern British Columbia remained essentially unexplored. At a time when Montreal and Toronto were emerging as important cities in Eastern Canada even the fundamental physical features of mountains and rivers remained almost unknown in northern British Columbia.

Despite the modest beginnings in forestry, mining, and agriculture in the southwest, population in the new province was small. British Columbia's entry into Confederation in 1871 had no obvious immediate effects upon the economy of the coastal settlements, and it did not halt the economic and population decline of the interior until railway construction started in the 1880s. The census of 1881 recorded only about 24,000 Europeans, plus an estimated 25,000 native Indians. The Pacific position of the province was illustrated by the census report of more Chinese (4,350) than either Scottish (3,900) or Irish (3,200).

In 1881 Victoria, the capital and largest city, plus its adjoining agricultural hinterland on Saanich peninsula, held almost 30 percent of the European population (about 7,000 persons). New Westminster had about 3,000 people and was the "central place" and largest town of the Lower Fraser Valley. Victoria was still the main port of entry for the province in 1881; imported goods in that year were valued at about two million dollars, in comparison with 320,000 dollars worth of imports through New Westminster. Exports also moved through Victoria coming mainly from the mainland or up-coast. These exports, led by coal from Nanaimo, were nearly all raw materials — gold, seal furs, fish and animal products, indicating the resource-based economy of the province. By 1881 Victoria had diversified its economy by adding numerous (169) small manufacturing establishments; a small industrial area had arisen on the north side of the city along the harbour. (Map No. 5, p. 21)

New Westminster was the main commercial centre of the Low-

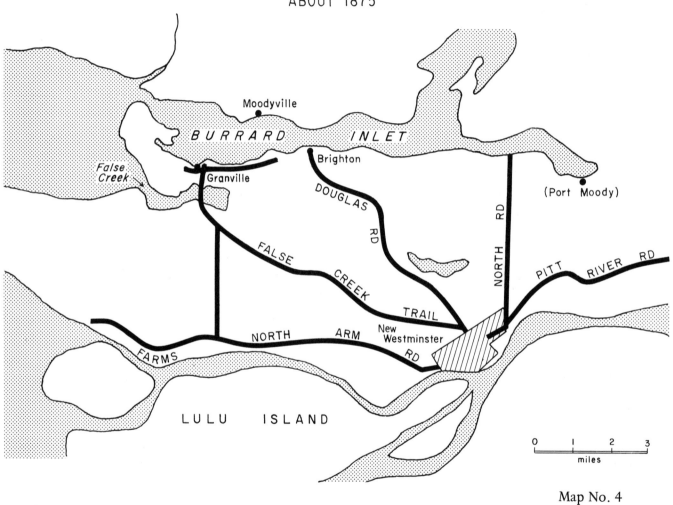

EARLY SETTLEMENTS AND ROADS
IN THE BURRARD - FRASER REGION
ABOUT 1875

Moodyville

BURRARD INLET

Brighton

False Creek

Granville

DOUGLAS RD

(Port Moody)

NORTH RD

FALSE

PITT RIVER RD

CREEK

TRAIL

New Westminster

FARMS

NORTH ARM RD

LULU ISLAND

0   1   2   3
miles

Map No. 4

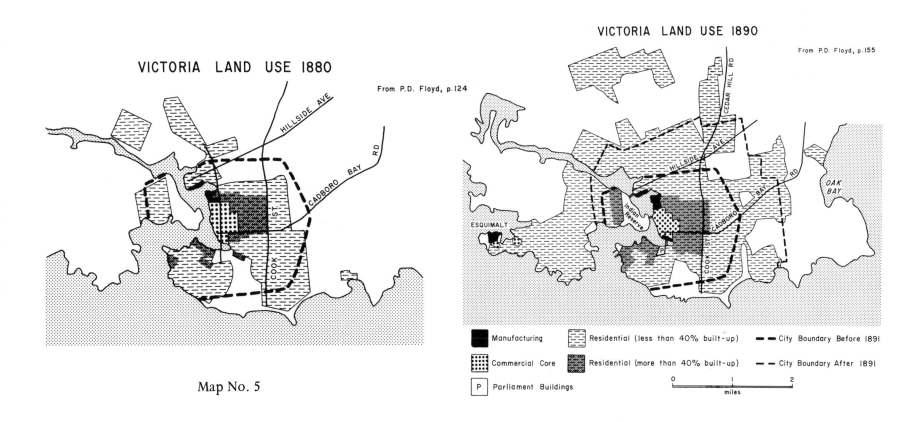

VICTORIA LAND USE 1880

From P.D. Floyd, p.124

HILLSIDE AVE

CADBORO BAY RD

COOK ST.

Map No. 5

VICTORIA LAND USE 1890

From P.D. Floyd, p.155

CEDAR HILL RD

HILLSIDE AVE

OAK BAY

ESQUIMALT

Indian Reserve

P

CADBORO BAY RD

COOK ST.

■ Manufacturing   ▦ Residential (less than 40% built-up)   ▬ ▬ City Boundary Before 1891

▦ Commercial Core   ▨ Residential (more than 40% built-up)   — — City Boundary After 1891

P Parliament Buildings

0   1   2
miles

21

er Mainland in 1881. Its stores along Columbia Street supplied the increasing number of farmers settling along the north arm of the Fraser River and on the nearby fertile delta soils. New Westminster was connected by rough roads through the heavy forest to its hinterland settlements northward on Burrard Inlet. For example, Brighton, later named Hastings (and now is Hastings Park in Vancouver), was a hotel and resort for picnics and recreation for the residents of New Westminster. Possibly 2,000 persons resided around Burrard Inlet, mainly in or near the sawmill towns of Moodyville and Granville. These several settlements were the nucleii of what was to become metropolitan Vancouver. (Map No. 4, p. 20)

Post~Confederation Speculation: 1886~1918

The anticipated arrival of the transcontinental railway through the Fraser Valley to Burrard Inlet heralded the founding of Vancouver in 1886. This arrival doomed the dominance of Victoria, foretelling the emergence of Vancouver as the primate centre of the Georgia Strait region and of British Columbia. The building of the Canadian Pacific Railway stimulated further exploration of the resource potential of the province, which, in turn, encouraged a major influx of speculative capital.

The arrival of the railway changed the relative location of the region. Prior to 1871 British Columbia was an isolated British colony 14,000 sea miles from the mother country; after 1886 it became a far-off province 2500 miles by rail across the Canadian Shield and Prairies from the heart of Eastern Canada. At the same time its ties with western United States were strengthened, particularly by railways built northward into the Kootenay mining region in the southeast.

The search for a route for the Canadian Pacific Railway through the Cordillera illustrated the lack of knowledge at that time of the extent of the mountain ranges, and particularly of the character of potential passes through the valleys. (Map No. 10, p. 34) When one realizes the vast accumulation of physical environmental knowledge which precedes present-day road building one has to marvel at the success of the railway-builders who knew so little about the British Columbia environment. These builders were not particularly interested in selecting a rail route to develop local resources; they wished mainly to find a series of linking valleys which would connect the prairie line with a west coast terminal. One of the routes considered was along Bute Inlet, crossing Georgia Strait at Seymour Narrows to reach Vancouver Island. Such a route, with Victoria as a terminal, might have maintained that city's economic dominance. However, this was not to be, and the Fraser Valley route was chosen. Despite the construction problems of carving a rail line into the steep walls above the Thompson and Fraser rivers, this latter valley route had the best grades through the Coast Mountains. In addition, it led to coastal towns and facilities which were already established and known to some world shipping. In a sense, the railway did not establish new geographical patterns on the coast, it simply accelerated the areal expansion of some of the established patterns. The arrival of the long-awaited railway had a greater immediate economic impact upon the Georgia Strait region than upon the interior.

Coastal British Columbia

Granville had become Vancouver in 1886 and was chosen as the site for the railway station and for the wharves which were to connect with ocean shipping. When Port Moody was named as the original railway terminal it had its land boom in 1884-85 and became another settlement nucleus on Burrard Inlet. But shallow water in its harbour, and tricky currents at the Second Narrows, were reminders that environmental conditions should not be overlooked in political decisions. The railway terminal in Vancouver was a mile west of the Hastings sawmill, which had been attracting deepsea ships to Burrard Inlet for more than a generation. The new city was laid out over a large area in anticipation of its role as Canada's "Gateway to the Pacific." Its southern boundary, along present-day 16th Avenue, was far south of any expected residential settlement near the harbour. Vancouver was the fourth of the major urban places to be established around Georgia Strait, following Victoria, Nanaimo, and New Westminster.

It was supported by the railway, some small sawmills, and hope.

The railway, a "growth" industry of the time, was the catalyst. It provided a means for hundreds of entrepreneurs and workers to come west to make their fortunes. In retrospect one wonders what the specific attractions of Vancouver were at that time: the natural resources of the coast were not yet well known; it is doubtful if its mild climate had an economic appeal then. Perhaps the city's growth was simply part of the general lure of the western frontier. One can surmise that men of that time thought in geographical terms and were confident that a city of size was inevitable at the end of rail on the west coast. Large infusions of speculative capital from Eastern Canada, Britain, and the United States were invested in street railways, one of the first modern electrical systems, stores, hotels, docks and lumber mills. Wholesale, transport, financial and service functions— which soon rivalled those in Victoria— were also established, reflecting the bouyant view of the future. Vancouver took advantage of its relative position between Victoria and the interior to capture the trade area of the mainland and also the resources frontier northward along the coast. A momentum was established that neither fire, scarcity of labour nor intercity rivalry could slow.

Vancouver's internal geographical patterns of urban land uses were established firmly in its first two decades of areal growth. The commercial core of Water, Cordova, Carrall, Main and Hastings streets occupied the site of old Granville. Two-storey, wooden houses on narrow lots spread east of Main Street and south of Hastings Street to a much larger (than now), shallow False Creek. The larger and "nicer" homes were built in the west end of the city, west of Burrard Street. The railway occupied the edge of the harbour; along it were established warehouses, lumber mills, fish canneries and other industries. A second industrial area was to arise around False Creek after 1890, dominated by numerous sawmills.

Victoria, the capital, remained the largest city in the province for another decade. In 1891, its population— in part British immigrants and some American entrepreneurs— remained small, totalling about 17,000. Because it was the chief port of the province it received the initial benefits of increased trade which followed the completion of the Canadian Pacific Railway. The building of the Esquimalt-Nanaimo railway in 1886 further focused Vancouver Island products and trade through Victoria. Through a few strong individuals Victoria increased its dominance over commerce, trade and government of all of British Columbia. For example, capital from Victoria built some of the fish canneries at the mouth of the Skeena River. Victoria's merchants maintained commercial connections in western United States that were as significant as their personal and political ties with Britain. Similar to San Francisco of that period, Victoria had an established elite some of whom were second-generation British Columbians. Their political and social connections with the small settlements which revived in the interior were fostered and strengthened. Victoria's private schools, run on the British tradition, attracted the ablest young men from the mainland. The stately homes of Oak Bay, to arise later on the eastern edge of Victoria, were symbolic of this rooted society.

Victoria attained its height as the dominant urban centre of British Columbia in about 1891. New wharfs were built, the commercial core expanded, and renewal on Douglas Street saw large, stone or brick buildings bring an air of permanence there. Victoria was the third city in Canada to introduce electric street cars in 1890, and these encouraged and directed the outward areal expansion of residential areas. (Map No. 5, p. 21) As in other cities of the time, residential segregation related to economic or social status, or to ethnic or cultural backgrounds, was apparent in the city's landscape. For example, about 2,000 Chinese were highly concentrated in the area near Cormorant and Fisgard streets. (Map No. 2, p. 16)

About half of British Columbia exports moved through Victoria in 1891. These included fish products from the Fraser River canneries, fur seals from the North Pacific, coal from

Nanaimo, forest products from southeastern Vancouver Island, and gold from the mainland interior. Victoria was still the main manufacturing city of the province, recording 245 industrial establishments (many were small) with 2100 employees in 1891. For example, more than half of the provincial workers in clothing establishments and construction industries were in Victoria.

Despite the relative commercial and industrial growth of Victoria, its direct hinterland remained small and sparsely populated. Only a few thousand persons had cleared farmland on adjoining Saanich peninsula where 32,000 acres were cultivated in 1891. The only other settlement of the region was at Esquimalt where about 350 persons resided.

By 1901 Vancouver had become the largest city on the west coast. Its population of almost 30,000 persons had been achieved in 15 years, whereas Victoria had only about 21,000 people after 58 years of occupation. Vancouver's growth was not sure and steady nor particularly firmly based in its early years. In particular, the expansion of productive primary enterprises was slow. A false security based on sustained imports of capital was bolstered briefly by the Klondike gold rush of 1898. For a time Vancouver competed with Victoria and Seattle for the position of gateway to the Yukon goldfields.

In retrospect, one now wonders about the optimistic expectations of the impact of the new railway; the increase in freight traffic was small and cannot be interpreted as a prime driving force in the community. In the port of Vancouver lumber shipments abroad continued at a similar volume as before the city was founded. Even when trans-Pacific liner service was established only passengers and mail, and minor inbound cargoes of tea, matting, porcelain, and silk, passed into the port. In total, the effects of the hinterland of British Columbia upon Vancouver were small prior to 1900, and the amount of freight generated by the railway through the port was not in proportion to the rapid increase in population in the city. Grain shipments from the Prairies to Vancouver were not significant before World War I; the Prairies were hardly settled in 1900; and in any case their markets were eastward. Undoubtedly the opening of several mines in southeastern British Columbia after 1890 affected commerce and finance in Vancouver, but freight to and from that region did not pass through Vancouver until after the Kettle Valley railway was completed to the coast during World War I.

In the decade 1901-11 Vancouver's population increased by 91,000 persons, comparable to the population growth of 163,000 in Toronto during the same period. This growth was partly the result of local increases in primary production and processing in forestry and fisheries, and partly was related to a population spillover from the great migration to the prairies. As Vancouver increased in population the city itself provided an important consuming market. Growth was aided by speculation by a new entrepreneurial class in land, forests, utilities, shipping and fisheries. The tallest office building in the British Empire, the Dominion Bank Building, was built in these years, a symbol of the optimism of the period. Vancouver's commercial core expanded westward of the original centre in present-day "Gastown", and spread southward to link up with the commercial area adjacent to the C.P.R. hotel at Granville and Georgia streets. By this time street cars of the "Fairview Beltline" were serving stores and businesses on the circular route of Hastings, Granville, Broadway and Main streets. (Map No. 6, p. 26) The False Creek industrial area had become the major concentration of sawmills by about 1911. False Creek was an arm off English Bay but could not be used by deep-sea shipping because of the railway trestle blocking the entrance and shallow water in its eastern part; the area was, however, excellent for log booms. (Map No. 7, p. 27)

The outward areal expansion of homes to the west and east accelerated after 1900. Residences also spread south of False Creek, which was crossed by three bridges, and houses soon filled in most of the political area of the city to its boundary

COMMERCIAL AREAS OF VANCOUVER ABOUT 1913

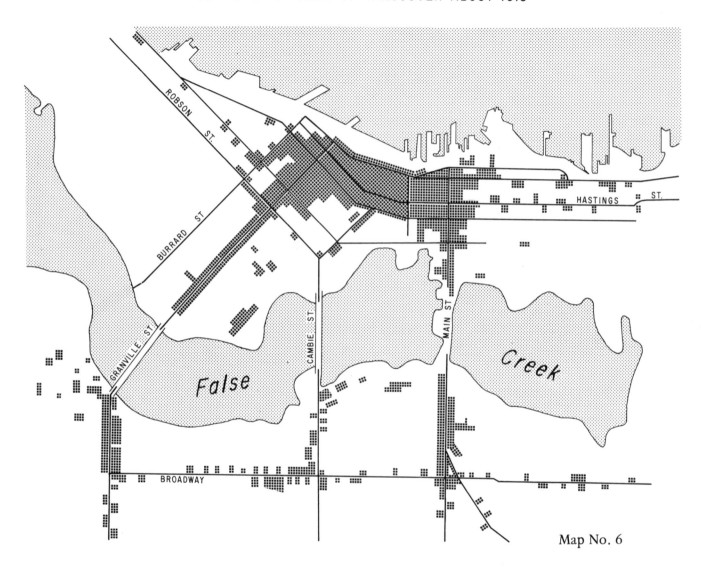

Map No. 6

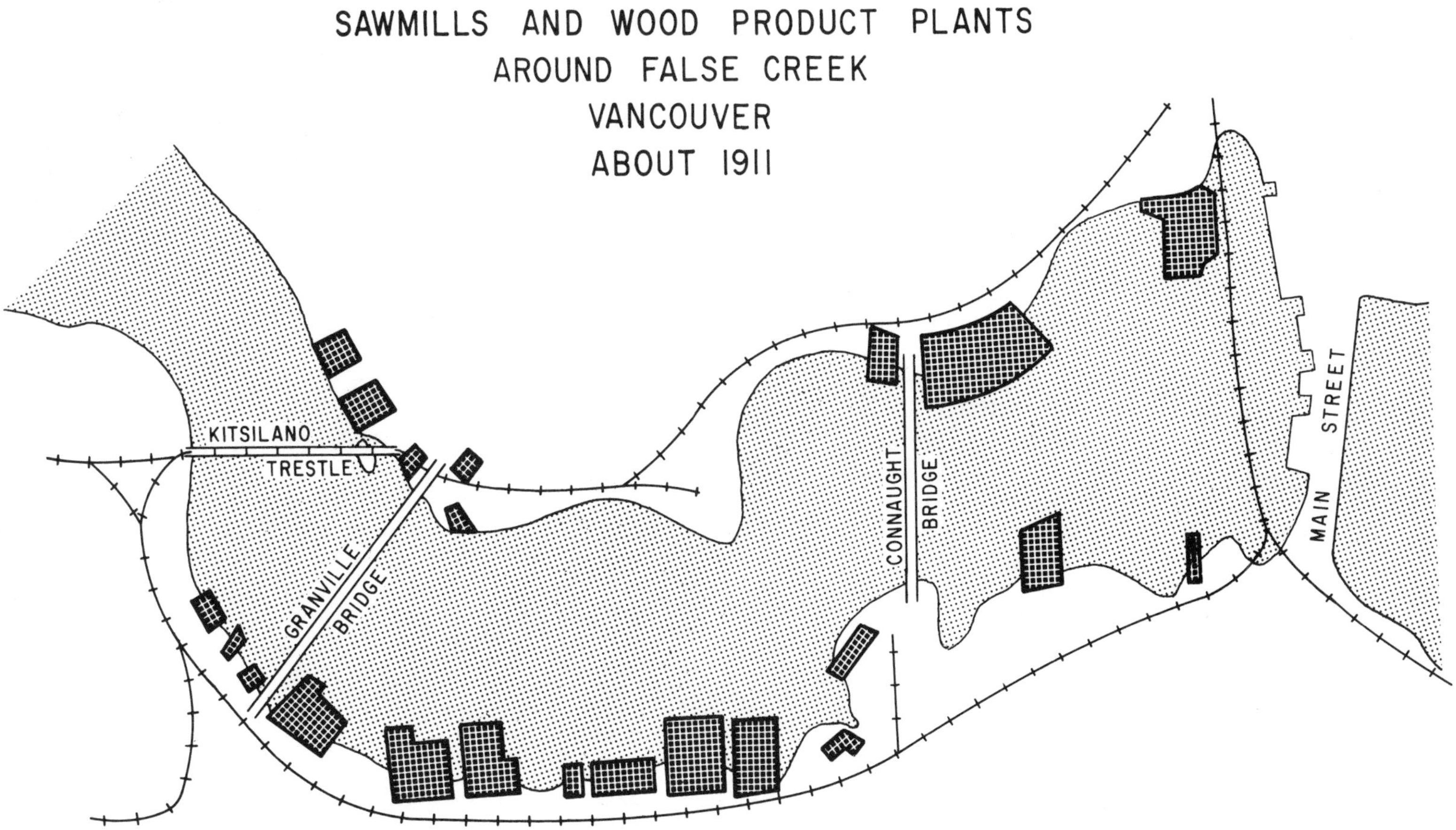

SAWMILLS AND WOOD PRODUCT PLANTS
AROUND FALSE CREEK
VANCOUVER
ABOUT 1911

KITSILANO
TRESTLE

GRANVILLE BRIDGE

CONNAUGHT BRIDGE

MAIN STREET

Map No. 7

along 16th Ave. By 1910 most of the West End peninsula was fully occupied to the edge of Stanley Park; the Kitsilano district, aided by the 4th Ave. street car line, was being settled after 1905. To the east the Grandview and Woodlands suburbs were opened in 1904 and the former was rapidly occupied by small houses by 1912. Commercial Drive, on the route of the interurban railway to New Westminster, was already a suburban shopping street for people in the East End. Hastings townsite, on the eastern boundary of the city was annexed in 1911, and was connected by a discontinuous strip of commercial use along Hastings Street. (Map No. 8, p. 29)

At the same time, urban functions were being established in South Vancouver. This rural municipality, on the south side of Burrard peninsula, was incorporated in 1892 and had several separate urban nucleii. It absorbed some of the first "suburban sprawl" of residents who built homes out in the second growth forest of the glacial uplands "to get away from" the congested city core. For example, residences spread to the southeast along the interurban rail line through South Burnaby to New Westminster; small commercial clusters arose along this route at major stops, such as the "village" known as Collingwood at Joyce Road. Other commercial strips followed the street car lines south on Victoria, Fraser and Main streets. The patterns of commercial land use were closely associated with street car lines throughout Vancouver and many of these were established prior to 1920.

In 1908 the people west of Cambie St. separated themselves from South Vancouver and formed the municipality of Point Grey. Their community goals and resulting urban landscapes were different from those of the people living eastward in South Vancouver. Point Grey included several large Canadian Pacific Railway land grants. In 1910 the C.P.R. began selling lots in the planned subdivision of Shaughnessy, on high land looking north over the city. Some of the large and stately homes were built on the large view lots prior to 1914, but many more were added in the 1920s. "Old" Shaughnessy was by no means fully occupied when the C.P.R. opened an-

other first class residential area south of King Edward Street in 1922, thereby establishing a sector of expensive homes southward on both sides of Granville Street. Many of the social and managerial elite of Vancouver moved from the West End to Shaughnessy, where the symbols of success were the mansions erected around The Crescent. Elsewhere in Point Grey a small "village" was arising in Kerrisdale where 41st Ave. crossed the interurban railway to Marpole and Richmond. The present-day Marpole district started as a small community known as Eburne, clustered around the sawmills and fish canneries on both sides of the Fraser River where a bridge crossed to Sea Island. Thus by 1918 the political limits of Vancouver of that time were fairly well occupied with distinct areas of residential, commercial and industrial land uses; and outside of Vancouver other communities were established which were to coalesce in a few decades into metropolitan Vancouver. (Map No. 8, p. 29)

But Vancouver had grown too fast. The minor increases in forestry and fishery production prior to 1914 were not proportionate to the city's vast commercial and residential expansion. Only 135,000 people lived in the resources hinterland of the mainland which supplied Vancouver. Although only one-quarter of the population of British Columbia lived in Vancouver in 1911, 66 percent of the population was concentrated in the Georgia Strait region consisting of eastern Vancouver Island, the Lower Fraser Valley and metropolitan Vancouver. The hinterland needed development. The effects of the mining booms in the Kootenays and in the Yukon declined early in the century. Competition from nearby American producers for lumber sales in the prairies became acute and profits decreased. The speculative economy, based partly on anticipated future rewards, slowed down noticeably. The crash was severe. In 1913 people began leaving Vancouver— if they could afford to. Hundreds of buildings were vacated, and subdivided lots in the suburbs became valueless. Then came the war, and young men of British ancestry, and others, left with the army for overseas. It was estimated that Vancouver's population decreased by a remark-

APPROXIMATE EXTENT OF URBAN OCCUPATION
AROUND 1910

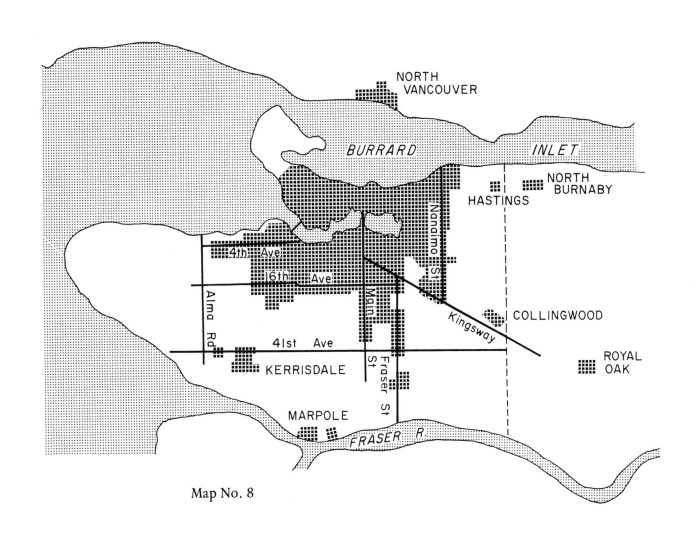

Map No. 8

able 20 percent from 122,000 in 1912 to 96,000 in 1916.

The Natural Resource Base

The increase in number and size of sawmills in Vancouver prior to 1914 reflected in part the increasing demand for lumber in the Prairie Provinces and in the city itself. When the forests around Burrard Inlet had been cut loggers moved north along the coast and also increased the cutting of the vast forest on the lowland of eastern Vancouver Island. The owners of large sawmills in Vancouver and along the Fraser River developed a log-towing system which brought logs from around Georgia Strait to the urban mills from whence there was ocean or rail transport to external markets. Coastal British Columbia was still far from world lumber markets, however, and the forest industry was partly a speculative one, with much buying and selling of forest land and leases.

The salmon canning industry was established along the coast at the turn of the century, with a large concentration of canneries near the mouth of the Fraser River, a smaller group on

the Skeena and Nass estuaries and isolated canneries along
the central coast. The two, three and four year cycles of the
various species of salmon had been known to the Indians for
generations, and Europeans made use of this seasonal abun-
dance after settlement. Because of the perishability of the
salmon and the lack of mobility and range of the fishing boats,
the canneries had to be located near the mouths of each spawning river. Cannery operations were often restricted to a few
weeks annually, and the fishing settlements might be unoccupied during the winter. The line of dispersed coastal canneries, like the logging camps, received their supplies and equipment from Vancouver, and in turn, shipped the canned salmon
to that city for export by ship or rail. Early in the century,
therefore, Vancouver had strengthened its position as the supply and commercial centre for the scattered and small coastal
settlements to the northward.

The increasing urban population created a market for nearby
agricultural products. The broad delta of the Fraser River and
the lowland of eastern Vancouver Island were the only relatively large areas of level land in coastal British Columbia, (except for the unoccupied lowland on the northeastern side of
the Queen Charlotte Islands), and their location near the urban consuming area certainly influenced the type of crop
grown. The Fraser delta floodplain was cleared, drained and
dyked; an agricultural economy evolved which produced
dairy products, meat, poultry, fruit and vegetables for Vancouver residents. Small villages arose along the river and
along the Canadian Pacific railway to serve the Fraser Valley
farms. The "upland" of the old glacial delta— about 200 to
300 feet above the modern delta— was generally unoccupied
because of its coarser soils and heavy forest cover. After 1910
when the B.C. Electric railway crossed the uplands south of
the river en route to Chilliwack, a new rural settlement pattern evolved in the Valley.

The Northern Coast

Similar to the situation of Vancouver, the city of Prince Rupert was established prior to World War I as a railway termin-
us; it also experienced a speculative boom. The building of
the Grand Trunk Pacific Railway west from Edmonton
through the upper Fraser, Bulkley and Skeena valleys in 1907-
1914 was meant to give Canada a second gateway through the
Cordillera to the Pacific Coast. The optimism shown in the
vast plans for Prince Rupert was not as well founded as that
for Vancouver; the population remained small. Port activities
and fisheries were established there but the city did not develop hinterland connections; ships calling at Prince Rupert had
fewer chances for a variety of cargoes. The strengthening of
the fish canning industry was one of the few bright spots in
Prince Rupert's economy. By 1918 there were 13 canneries
along the Skeena River estuary and another 5 canneries operated near the Nass mouth. Despite being "closer to the Orient" because of its northern location, Prince Rupert did not

become a second major west coast port.

While the northern railway was being constructed, and afterwards, there was speculation along the interior route in land and timber by American and eastern Canadian capitalists. Some forestry and agriculture were established, but there were few local markets and the area remained far from world consumers. Small villages were settled from the west in the Bulkley and Nechako valleys, but no communities of any size arose until after World War I. In 1913 many lumber mills along the northern railway line, like those of coastal southwestern British Columbia, were forced to close.

Interior
British Columbia

While Vancouver was asserting its dominance on the coast, resource development was renewed in certain sections of the interior. During the railway construction period of the 1880s some local agriculture and forestry became established to feed construction workers and supply timber needs. Ranching was revitalized across the dry grasslands from the northern Okanagan Valley to the area around Williams Lake. Man began to change the natural environment of the arid Okanagan Valley by bringing irrigation water to the terraces above the lake. Orchards were laid out near Vernon and southward. Several small settlements arose along the railroad, but no large communities emerged. The largest, Kamloops and Revelstoke, had 3,800 and 3,000 persons, respectively in 1911; the former grew very little in the next two decades, whereas the latter declined in population.

During the 1890s mineral discoveries brought the first large numbers of permanent population to the Kootenay and Boundary regions of southeastern British Columbia. Mining was the impetus for the introduction of transportation facilities and also created a demand for associated forestry and water power developments. Prospectors, mainly from the United States, moved northward along the valleys from the mining towns of western Montana and Idaho. Several gold or base metal mines were brought into production near the United States boundary, from Greenwood and Grand Forks on the west to the shores of Kootenay Lake on the east. Coal mining developed in the Crows Nest pass of the southern Rocky Mountains, with Fernie as the major city and supply centre for the mines (population estimate of 3,200 in 1911). In the West Kootenays the major cities were Nelson (4,500 population) and Rossland (1,700) in 1911. These small cities provided the main urban amenities for the region. In the early part of the 20th century the mineral wealth of the Canadian Shield in Eastern Canada was generally unknown and British Columbia was the leading mineral producing province in Canada; much of this production came from the southeast. (Map No. 9, p. 33)

The linear pattern of the mountain systems in the southeast— i.e. north-south ridges of the Purcell, Selkirk and Monashee Ranges — made east-west transport lines difficult. (Map No. 10, p. 34) The Kootenay River valley became an important route between Kootenay Lake settlements and those in the Columbia River valley. Internal movement was provided by large and small lake vessels on the Arrow Lakes and Kootenay Lake. However, the exploitation of large ore bodies required transportation to external markets. Short branch rail lines were built northward across the American border and the copper, lead, zinc, silver and other minerals moved southward to the Great Northern, and other, railways in the United States.

Numberous mining towns arose, flourished and sometimes died within a few years. The Kootenays went through a colourful mining boom similar to that which has been much better publicized in the mining camps of the American moun-

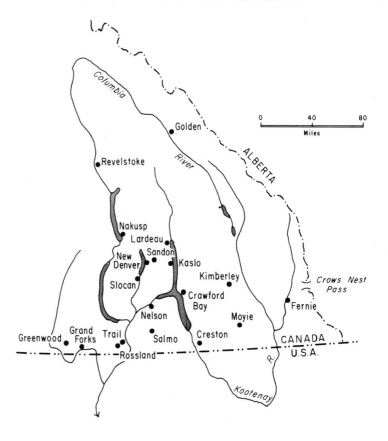

MINING CENTRES OF THE KOOTENAYS

Map No. 9

LANDFORM REGIONS OF BRITISH COLUMBIA

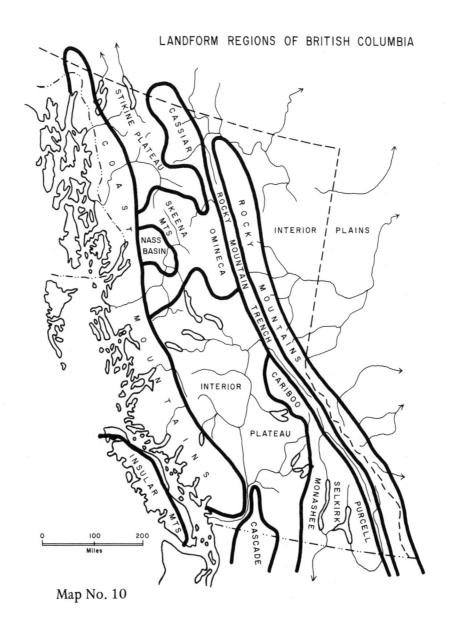

Map No. 10

tains to the southward. The towns sprawled on the lower slopes of mountains around the mine openings. Being built of wood, many of them decayed rapidly after abandonment or were burned down by carelessness. Places like Phoenix and Cascade City almost literally disappeared. At other centres such as Greenwood and Slocan scars of slag heaps and deteriorating smelters were left to awaken the memory of the modern tourist. At Grand Forks, for example, the mining economy which created the town is completely gone, but the city is now growing again, based on forestry. These scattered mining communities required local food production. As a result small farms were cleared in the narrow river valleys, on flood plains or side-valley terraces. But they were never able to produce sufficient food for the urban centres.

The fear of economic and political domination of southeastern British Columbia by American interests resulted in the construction of a southern line of the Canadian Pacific Railway just north of the United States boundary. This railway, completed during World War I, helped to direct the flow of ores westward to Vancouver and also gave the sawmills of the southeast an outlet eastward to new markets in the growing Prairie towns. Aided by the railway, and mining company reorganizations, the city of Trail showed the first indications of its future industrial importance in the West Kootenays. It was founded in 1890 as a ferry ramp and transfer warehouses were built for ore from Rossland that was carried down the steep slopes above the Columbia River and sent south to the United States. Gradually a small town grew up on the narrow terraces above Trail Creek, and the industrial character of Trail was established when a smelter was built north of the town on an upper terrace. By 1911 Trail had 1,500 persons and was competing in commercial functions with the nearby mining town of Rossland.

In the first decade of this century, with mines flourishing, sawmills humming, water power sites supplying power, and towns growing up at the transport centres, the southeast was important in the total economy of British Columbia. This

relative significance was never matched in future decades. Many of its functional links were southward to the United States or eastward to Alberta. Even to the present the southeastern part of British Columbia is not as closely connected economically to Vancouver as are the other southern and central areas.

By the end of World War I the major geographical patterns of economic activity were fairly well established in British Columbia. The Georgia Strait region, with its urban population, industries and commerce held more than half of the people in the Cordillera. Southeastern British Columbia had shown the beginnings of integrated resource development, but this momentum was not to be continued in the inter-war period to follow. Settlement was still scanty in the remainder of the Cordillera and was confined to the few valleys where there was transportation. The opening of the Panama Canal during the war was to change again the relative position of this region with regard to eastern Anglo-America and Europe.

The Period of Production Expansion: 1919~1946

The rapid increase in the rate of economic growth in the 1920s in British Columbia was based upon massive expansion in productivity, particularly in the forest industry. New markets for forest products were found, particularly in eastern United States and Europe. Forestry expansion— both in areal terms and in corporate structure— was aided by the creation of aggressive marketing firms, a new Canadian-operated shipping fleet, improved harvesting and transporting techniques, and new inflows of capital. Most economic expansion took place in the previously established industries of the Georgia Strait region, but in addition new settlements arose in the interior. A division of labour between the two major urban areas of the southwest became evident, with Victoria providing governmental services, and Vancouver the commercial and financial leadership.

On the Coast

The coastal forest industry expanded areally and increased production. At the same time that cutting activities expanded northward there was a concentration of sawmills and other wood processing plants in cities around Georgia Strait. A functional system of forestry was beginning to evolve. Logging camps were opened northward along the coast. New pulp mills at Powell River and Ocean Falls were dots of permanent industry on the sparsely-populated central coast. Logs were towed from as far away as the Queen Charlotte Islands. Logging railroads and roads gave access to the vast timber lands covering eastern Vancouver Island. By the late 1930s most of the coastal forest was either being cut into directly or was reserved for future expansion. There was some concern being voiced that this natural resource was being exploited too rapidly and that the forest would soon be exhausted, and with it would go one of the important bases of the coastal economy. Undoubtedly, man was changing the natural environment of large areas of vegetation on the coast, and a new geographical network of utilization centres was being created.

Fish catches also increased during this period; fishing and canning technology and vessels improved. When fishing vessels achieved a greater catching range it was no longer necessary to operate salmon canneries near the mouths of most coastal rivers. The number of canneries along the central coast therefore decreased, and the larger canneries expanded their operations near the mouths of the Fraser and Skeena rivers. From a maximum of 90 canneries along the coast in 1910-15, there was a reduction to 29 canneries in 1945. Decreases in numbers, increases in size, shifts from dispersal to concentration— all of these trends were changes in the geographical patterns of the fishing industry.

In Vancouver the port functions took on greater importance as a result of the Panama Canal which reduced distances to the North Atlantic consuming areas. Grain elevators were constructed and Alberta became part of the grain hinterland of Vancouver. Oil refineries were erected in the unoccupied eastern part of Burrard Inlet and supplied with crude oil by tankers from California. Sawmills moved from the valuable land of the Burrard Inlet harbour, and by the late 1930s were decreasing in number in the False Creek area; most of the large lumber mills were located along the Fraser River, extending from the Marpole area to the east beyond New Westminster. Whereas the port at Vancouver had previously been considered mainly as a gateway to the Orient, this Pacific trade did not develop as was hoped. Exporters therefore had to begin thinking in different geographical terms when it became apparent that the chief markets of British Columbia were in eastern Anglo-America and in northwestern Europe.

The increases in industry, trade, and particularly the concentration of management in Vancouver supported the rapidly growing population whose residences spread over most of Burrard peninsula and eastward into adjoining Burnaby. In 1929 Vancouver, South Vancouver and Point Grey were united into one large city with a 1931 population of 247,000. The functional unity and interconnections of Vancouver and its other suburban cities were well established in this inter-war period.

North Vancouver, incorporated in 1891, had evolved as a smaller replica of Vancouver, to which it was linked by frequent ferry service across the harbour. North Vancouver was supported by a few industries along its harbour before and after World War I. A small commercial strip grew northward along Lonsdale Ave., and paralleled the harbour along Marine Drive. Small homes for workers spread back from the harbour and slowly inched up the lower slopes. By 1931 North Vancouver had 8,500 residents and many of them were commuting by ferry across the harbour to jobs in the commercial and industrial core of downtown Vancouver.

For two decades West Vancouver consisted of a few homes along quiet Marine Drive and a small village centered near the ferry dock at Ambleside. The area was often a pleasant retreat for picnics at the end of the ferry ride from Vancouver. The population of 4,800 persons in 1931 had no local industrial base except for those employed in a few local stores. Much of this pleasant suburban life was to change after 1938 when the Lions Gate bridge made it possible for business and professional men to build new homes in West Vancouver and then commute by car (in addition to the ferries) to the commercial core of nearby Vancouver. This bridge, like other transportation links — short and long — in British Columbia, was to change the geographical patterns of residence and "journey to work" of people working in commerce and business in downtown Vancouver. In particular, the opening of the British Properties superior residential area on the middle slope above Capilano River, gave Vancouver's wealthy a new place in which to concentrate. This movement was similar in function to the opening of the Shaughnessy area 20 years previously.

By 1941 Vancouver had 275,000 population, and there were almost 100,000 persons in the adjoining municipalities. The metropolitan area was well established as the third largest city in Canada. Vancouver itself contained the most important places of work in the urban area. Workers commuted to these industrial and commercial areas which were in the same general zones as in 1920. Those who lived in the municipalities outside of Vancouver could still experience the flavour of "rural" living which was to be gone from those places 20 years later.

In the Interior

While production was increasing in coastal British Columbia there was also an expansion in resource-oriented activities in the interior. Agricultural settlement was scattered in valleys across the southern part of the province near transport lines, but none of it compared in cultivated area or importance with the agriculture of the Lower Fraser Valley near urban Vancouver. In the Okanagan Valley the area of irrigated fruit and vegetable farms increased after 1920 and this valley emerged as a major interior producer of agricultural crops. Compared with the 1880s, man saw the natural environment of the Okanagan Valley in a different way in the 1920s and 1930s; he then had the technology and desire to change this environment to produce new crops. Irrigation water could be led down in flumes to the small farms on the narrow, former glacial lake terraces. Apple trees in particular were planted, starting near Vernon; their fruit had a ready market in the towns of the Prairie Provinces where European settlers liked apples but could not grow them.

The areal distribution of irrigation spread southward in the Okanagan Valley. Rural population densities increased in the side valleys near Vernon, spread across the semicircular basin east of Kelowna, and strung out along the white silt and kame terraces above Okanagan and Skaha lakes near Penticton. Many irrigation works were started as private projects, but ultimately most had to be taken over by local governments. In the dry southern Okanagan Valley, where annual precipitation was only about 10 inches, a government-sponsored irrigation project meant for soldier settlement brought intensive agriculture by the mid-1920s. The longer average frost-free season in the south encouraged the planting of the soft fruits such as apricot, cherry, peach, plum and pear. Thus the regional characteristics of the southern part of the Okanagan Valley were different from the northern sections. Occasional killing winter temperatures and a few devastating late spring frosts indicated, however, that the whole valley was on the climatic margins for soft fruit production. Despite the warnings of climatic hazards fruit acreage increased steadily; the surplus crop which could not be absorbed in western Canada was shipped to welcome markets in Britain.

A line of small service-centre cities grew up in the Okanagan Valley during this period. Early in the century both Vernon and Kelowna had fruit packing and processing plants which depended on external markets either in Vancouver, in the Prairies or later in Britain. Penticton established similar industries later, particularly after the Kettle Valley Railway (C.P.R.) to Vancouver was constructed through it in 1915. By 1941 the Okanagan Valley was the main area of almost continuous settlement in the interior with a regional population of 45,000. It had a mixture of small towns and small farms which was similar to the settlement pattern of the agricultural Lower Fraser Valley, although the two areas produced different types of crops. Although linked by rail to Vancouver, and dependent on external markets for its apples, the Okanagan Valley was generally a self-contained unit; it

was establishing its own internal areal patterns of utilization and residence.

There was little change in the settlement patterns in southeastern British Columbia or along the north coast during the inter-war period. A type of corporate integration took place among the mining companies of the Kootenays, similar to that which developed in the forest industry of the coast. At Kimberley, British Columbia's largest mine produced silver-lead-zinc and other by-product metals; the concentrates were transported by rail to Canada's largest base metals smelter, refinery and associated fertilizer plant at Trail. Ores also came to this smelter from as far away as the central Yukon, emphasizing the importance of the smelter in the functional operations of the mining industry. Although much of the processed ores and fertilizer of the southeast region moved west through Vancouver, its lumber moved eastward, illustrating the marginal position of the southeast region in Vanouver's hinterland.

Expansion in the central interior was mainly related to a developing forestry industry. Logging increased along the railroads, but throughout this inter-war period production of the whole interior was usually only about one-third of that on the coast. Mills were numerous, dispersed, and often small and portable; there was a division of labour between logger, sawmill and planer operator. North of the Chilcotin and Cariboo ranching districts there were only a few small sawmill towns, such as Quesnel and Prince George. The latter had a sawmill-based economy from the time of its founding in 1909. About 16 sawmills produced in, or near, Prince George in 1916 and 23 sawmills were reported there in 1926. The community was entirely dependent on the northern Canadian National Railway to move its lumber, although a rough road from southern British Columbia reached the town in 1924. In 1931 Prince George had 2,500 residents, and nearby Quesnel had 450 persons, indicating that they had only minor service and commercial functions at that time. The sawmill industry, and the population, declined during the depression years of the 1930s and the railway occupations and government services kept Prince George alive. During World War II a nearby army camp and a new airport revived commerce in the town, but the main expansion in the forest industry came in the 1950s when large markets were developed in central United States, to supplement the traditional Prairie outlets.

By 1940 the linear settlement patterns, which were railway and/or valley oriented, were well established in interior British Columbia. South of the main Canadian Pacific rail line several north-south valleys had different intensities of settlement and various occupations. The economy of each linear region was somewhat self-contained, although transport lines to other regions and to Greater Vancouver existed. To the northward settlement was in isolated clusters along the Pacific Great Eastern Railway to Quesnel, and along the northern Canadian National Railway to Prince Rupert. Away from these rail lines there was only a scattering of large ranches across the southern part of the Interior Plateau. The period of intensive resource development and population expansion in the interior was to come mainly after 1950. In contrast, integration of productive facilities in terms of corporate ownership and functional linkages was already apparent on the coast. Whereas the inter-war period was one of production expansion and urban growth in coastal British Columbia, it was a period when the beginnings of industry were being planted in the interior.

Industrial Growth and Functional Integration: 1946-1971

The increasing production recorded on the coast in the previous period became apparent in the southern and central interior after World War II. Much of this growth was the result of new markets and of new technology in industry and transportation. Greater functional integration of the Georgia Strait region with parts of the southern and central interior occurred in this post-war period. Greater Vancouver increased its dominance as the manufacturing, commercial and financial centre of the province. The resource potential of British Columbia was large enough to withstand the high costs of overcoming the disadvantage of mountain landforms, great distances and relatively small local markets. The resource-based economies which were greatly affected were forestry, mining and to a lesser extent, fisheries. Paralleling these developments was a greater use of electric energy.

Forestry

The horizontal and vertical integration of the forest industry resulted in the sawmills around Georgia Strait becoming very interdependent with other phases of wood production and product distribution. No longer was each logging camp and sawmill an isolated entity. These dispersed forestry operations were integrated by large corporations which added new production facilities. After about 1960 similar production and corporate trends became evident in the central and southern Interior. For example, MacMillan-Bloedel Limited has sawmills in Vancouver and Chemainus, a plywood and shingle mill at Vancouver, a kraft pulp mill near Nanaimo, and a newsprint mill at Powell River. The company's logging camps operate throughout the Coast forest from southern Vancouver Island to the Queen Charlotte Islands. Logs are sorted and graded at the camps and towed to the mill in which the log will be best utilized. Each major company has similar "linked" mills, and many smaller mills, in the Georgia Strait region. Integration is continuing. Throughout the forest industry efficient loggers use modern techniques and equipment, which are improved almost annually, and adapted to the environmental conditions of the West Coast forest, climate and landforms. The area around Georgia Strait is therefore one large interconnected forest-industry region, in which the separate operations of logging, transporting logs, processing, manufacturing of paper or wood products, and the provision of docks for export purposes or rail terminals, are all closely connected both in areal space and in corporate organization.

Some of the economic and distributional patterns of the coast forest industry are beginning to be repeated in the interior, but at an accelerated pace. Prince George is becoming of primate importance in a forest economy which is somewhat similar to that of the Georgia Strait region. Its cross-roads position, served by rail, road and pipeline, assisted its rise to dominance. The construction of three pulp mills at Prince George, plus two others within sixty miles, has prompted change. The installation of chippers for full utilization of wood waste, the centralization and increasing scale of sawmilling and improved efficiency of transport indicate a high level of integration.

Although forestry activities have made a most obvious impact upon the geographical patterns in the central Fraser River area, this type of resource-use expansion is also changing the local economies to the west in the Bulkley Valley and in the Terrace-Prince Rupert area, and throughout many valleys in south-central and southeast British Columbia. For example, forestry is now more valuable in the Kamloops area than is the traditional ranching industry. In the historic Boundary-Kettle Valley area, where mines supported a thriving economy early in this century, lumbering is now the main source of income and the chief employer among the primary industries. Grand Forks is an example of this change in resource-base. New pulp mills at Castlegar, in the Columbia River valley, and at Skookumchuk in the Rocky Mountain Trench, became markets for the previously wasted scrap wood of the sawmills in those areas, and also encouraged the harvesting of smaller trees.

Mining

The mining industry changed rapidly in the past decade as a result of increased demands for minerals, particularly in Japan and the United States. Although mines open and close and the dots on a mining map move, the Cordillera as a whole remains an important mining region. The Kootenays in the southeast continue to be the region of major production, but in the 1960s new mines dispersed throughout the Cordillera, reminiscent of the pattern and significance of mining at the turn of the century. The giant smelter-refinery-fertilizer complex at Trail is a focus for many of the metal mines of that region, particularly for their silver-lead-zinc ores. Further functional integration was illustrated by the opening of a pig iron plant at Kimberley, reprocessing the mineral waste collected for half a century outside the Sullivan mine.

The major mineral production of the southeast not dependent greatly on the facilities of the Trail smelter is the bituminous coal of the Fernie-Crowsnest Pass area in the Rocky Mountains. Coal production in this region declined after the late 1940s, as it did elsewhere in Canada. As a result of increased Japanese demand, however, and the introduction of strip-mining techniques and unit-car railway facilities, coal could be carried economically to new bulk-loading facilities near Vancouver for export to Japan. Changing geographical patterns are apparent to visitors to the Crowsnest Pass area; the new houses at Sparwood contrast to the small, dirty buildings at Michel; new stores, motels and houses at Fernie tell of its increased service functions for the region.

The new mining centres arising in British Columbia are dependent on markets and economic conditions in external consuming areas because local industrial markets in the Pacific Northwest are relatively small. Despite the visual attractiveness and apparent permanence of the new mining towns one must recall that the ghost towns of early in this century also depended on these external markets. The copper mines near Merritt, Logan and Ashcroft, on the plateau east of the Cascade Mountains, like new copper and iron mines on the coast, were brought into production after 1950 as a result of Japanese investment capital and markets. New molybdenum mines at Endako, near Peachland, Boss Mountain and Rossland, and the expansion of long-fibre asbestos production from Cassiar near the Yukon boundary, are all examples of the influence, and vulnerability, of external conditions.

The geographical distribution pattern of the 33 mines which were operating in 1971 is a little different from the areal distribution of the 30 mines which were in production in 1952. At both times slightly less than half of the operating mines were in the Kootenay region of the southeast. However, in 1952 there were more mines in the northwest than in 1971, but in this latter year there were more mines on the coast and in the central interior than 20 years ago. By 1971, one new mining region had been added to the map, with the discovery and production of petroleum and natural gas from the Peace River area. The many producing wells there have

brought changes to that formerly agriculturally-dominated economy, and the energy transported outward by pipelines has aided industries and heated homes in southwestern British Columbia and elsewhere. In the northwest, behind the Alaska Panhandle, mines have operated intermittently throughout much of this century; but production and development costs are high, and there is no local smelter. The favourable mineral potential of the area awaits future political decisions concerning greater freedom of accessibility across the international boundary, or the northwest extension of the British Columbia Railway (formerly the Pacific Great Eastern Railway) from Prince George. As in colonial days, policy decisions made outside of the region may determine the future use of these northern resources.

Fisheries & Agriculture

The geographical changes in these industries have not been as noticeable as in the other primary industries. The areal trend towards decreasing fish canneries and increasing size of the processing facilities, noted prior to 1940, accelerated in the past two decades. Most of these large fish canneries are now located near the mouths of the Fraser and Skeena rivers, and this processing activity has almost ceased along the central coast. Careful conservation measures, the control of fishing seasons and gear, and improvement in salmon spawning grounds and improved access to these spawning waters, have all helped to maintain salmon as a valuable, renewable natural resource. Less careful watching of the harvesting of herring resulted in almost depletion of this resource in the mid-1960s, and the curtailment of this segment of the fishing industry. In the coastal landscape the small fishing village has virtually disappeared; such settlements never were many nor large in British Columbia, unlike on the east coast of Canada. Most of the fishing fleet now rests between harvest seasons in, or near, Greater Vancouver or Prince Rupert.

The present areas of agricultural production were nearly all occupied prior to 1940. Unlike the serious trends in other parts of Canada, agricultural acreage and population are not decreasing rapidly in British Columbia. However, the total area of cultivated land — 1,614,000 acres in 1966, excluding ranchlands, is small and only equals that of the three Maritime Provinces; similarly, less than 5 percent of British Columbia's population is classed as agricultural. The most valuable agricultural production is in the Lower Fraser Valley, near the consuming market of Vancouver, but that increasing urban population is at the same time a reason for decreasing acreage in the western sections of the Valley as former dairy farms are subdivided into suburban residential areas. Improved road transportation after 1947 permitted the various agricultural regions of the province to become better integrated into the economy. For example, the completion of the Hope-Princeton highway gave access in a few hours to the Vancouver market for fruit and vegetable production of the Okanagan. On another scale, the completion of the P.G.E. railway to the Peace River area permitted feed grains from there to be brought directly to cattle-feeder lots in the Lower Fraser Valley. In the north-central interior farmland clearing is increasing along or near the northern C.N.R. line, partly as the result of improved road transport to markets, partly due to the larger local markets in cities such as Prince George, and partly the result of a minor "back to the land" movement of people who are moving to the "frontier" to get away from certain aspects of city life.

Electric Power

The increased pace of resource development has been aided by the availability and use of electric power. People in British Columbia have made good use of their vast hydro-power resources from the earliest days when technology made it available. For example, Victoria had electric lights for street illumination in 1882, just one year after Edison's developments in New York, and had a commercial hydro-power plant operating within two years of the first power power plant at Niagara Falls (1895). Vancouver was being supplied with electric power from Buntzen Lake in 1903, at a time when many towns in Eastern Canada were still without hydro-power. Electrolytic methods of refining lead were used at Trail early in this century after power dams were built on the Kootenay River in 1907. As Vancouver grew, the power demands of industry and homes were met by developing small hydro sites in the Coast Mountains nearby. In the inter-war period, as transmission technology improved, plants were con-

structed farther away, east of the mountains, such as at Bridge River. By 1940 hydro-power production was confined to the southwest, where most of the industry and people were, and to the Kootenay region to supply the metallurgical plant at Trail. During this time power production had expanded along with the demands of industry and of urban consumers, but it was not in itself a major attraction to new industry.

After about 1950 the role of electric power in economic development partially changed; its generation became a positive attraction for industry. For example, the diversion of the headwaters of the Nechako River through a tunnel under the Coast Mountains led to the generation of low-cost power for the Kitimat aluminum smelter in 1954. The raw materials, bauxite and alumina, were imported from the Caribbean, and thus industry came to a tide-water site where ample power was available. Throughout British Columbia hydro-electric power became a symbol of regional economic growth in the 1960s. All major rivers were studied for their potential. The Fraser River and its tributaries have a large water power potential, plus proximity to tide-water industrial sites and urban markets in southwestern B.C.; but the basin is also the most important salmon-spawning region in the province. The Fraser ser River Basin was therefore by-passed in the 1960s in favour of government-sponsored power dams on the Columbia and Peace rivers. One of the vexing future problems of "multiple-use" of resources will revolve around decisions as to how to make the "best" use of the water resources of the Fraser River Basin.

The damming of the Columbia River, a controversial political issue a decade ago, clouded by conflicting technical and economic evidence, became a reality after the signing of the Columbia River Treaty between Canada and the United States in 1964. The dams on the Columbia River in Canada were designed mainly for storage purposes, to improve power production at downstream plants in the United States. The water will not be directly producing electric power in British Columbia until turbines are installed at the Mica Creek dam in a few years. By the terms of the treaty British Columbia sold some of its rights to the Columbia River power and decided to produce additional power for provincial use from the Peace River. Aside from the inflow of capital through the provincial government, and the provision of temporary construction work during the building of the dams, the Columbia River power development has had little economic impact upon the southeast region.

The electric power produced from the Peace River has assisted local industries at Prince George in the central interior and in the northeast, but the main purpose of this power development was to supply electrical energy to the increasing market of Greater Vancouver 600 miles away. In contrast to conditions of two decades ago at Kitimat where low cost energy at tidewater offered an opportunity for an energy-intensive industry, electric power from the Peace River does not provide such a positive attraction to industry on the coast. For many industries other factors which influence the location of plants are now more significant than power. In addition the industries and urban residents of the southwest can now call upon the competing thermal power sources of petroleum and natural gas which were not available in 1950. The combined demands of markets in the Georgia Strait region and those in adjoining Washington State resulted in the construction of natural gas and petroleum pipelines from the Peace River area. These energy sources compete successfully with hydro-electric power, and in particular are useful supplements to hydro-electric power at times of peak load.

Water power developments have a geographical pattern in British Columbia. The first power plants were built in the southwest near the demand; as technology improved sites farther away could be developed. With major power sources operating in the four corners of the province — Peace River, Kemano, Columbia, Lower Mainland — no part of populated British Columbia is far from power developments. Undoubtedly, the resource-based industries throughout the province have been aided by having available electric power nearby.

Transportation in Regional Development

The integration of resource developments throughout central and southern British Columbia, and the closer linking of the coast and the interior, can be attributed to a variety of transportation improvements and additions. New roads were built in the interior and old roads were widened and paved. Linear distance could be measured more accurately in terms of time and cost distance. For example, the Okanagan Valley or Kamloops, formerly a long day away from Vancouver, is now only five or six hours away by highway. Williams Lake, once a small "cow-town" in the ranching area, has a large cluster of modern motels as a result of being 300 miles, an easy day's drive, from the Lower Mainland urban area. Even Prince George, considered by the pre-war generation as being "far-northern B.C." is only 500 miles away or one long day by car or truck or a brief flight by frequent air service. Improved access has had both positive and negative effects on the interior communities. For some, new roads have meant better access to markets and services and resultant population growth; for others the local service functions became less vital, illustrated by the closing of the small general stores and the rural schools.

Most of the towns of interior British Columbia grew up around the railway station; the commercial core was near the station and industries were along the railway. The improvement of highways, often built around the edge of the town, has resulted in internal changes in the patterns of local land use. For example, the traveller along the Trans-Canada highway may be impressed by the strip of new commercial buildings on the north side of Revelstoke, and may never see the old commercial core near the railway station. Similarly, a second commercial core, and new residential areas, opened at Fernie near the highway on the north side of the city and these contrast with the old buildings of the "downtown" area near the railway station. One is correctly impressed with the rapid growth in population at Kamloops and Prince George — both with excellent cross-roads geographical position — but may not be aware that there was no increase in population between 1966 and 1971 in Nelson, Rossland and Esquimalt and only minor increases in Chilliwack, Hope and Duncan.

The functional unity of the Georgia Strait region has been greatly assisted by the provision of excellent and frequent ferry services. These connect the urban centres around the Strait and give access to settlements on the central and north coast. The significance of Georgia Strait for the movement of industrial material, especially wood products, was noted in a preceding section. The ferry system is a "water highway" for the region and is focused on Vancouver, just as many of the interior highways funnel towards the Lower Fraser Valley. On the Vancouver-Victoria ferries salesmen, government officials, businessmen and tourists provide a stream of traffic that totals several thousand vehicles and passengers monthly; there is almost as much volume between West Vancouver and Nanaimo.

After the British Columbia Railway (formerly the Pacific Great Eastern) was connected to other rail lines in North Vancouver, and extended into the northeast and north-central parts of the province, it became one of the important north-south links, carrying resources, supplies and people between the interior and Greater Vancouver. It is not possible to assess accurately the economic impact of this provincial railway upon the interior economy and to separate its influence from that of other road and air connections, but the increased volumes and variety of its traffic leaves little doubt as to its value to the growth and integration of the provincial economy.

In the past two decades the revolution in transportation and communication has modified much of the feeling of isolation in British Columbia. Although distance and time have shrunk, the cost of these factors still affects the region. The mountains are not barriers to road and rail transport which follows the valleys, and in fact they attract many visitors to these road and rail lines. (Map No. 10, p. 34) Air transport flying at 20,000 to 30,000 feet is not greatly concerned whether there are mountains or plains below. Radio and television communication means that the Cordilleran settlements are in as close touch with the news and culture of the rest of the world as are any other parts of Canada. Just as transportation has brought the interior and the coastal parts of the province into greater functional unity, so are the economy and outlook of the people of British Columbia becoming more closely woven into the fabric of Canada.

The Landscape
as a Natural Resource

Whereas many interior and coastal resources move towards metropolitan Vancouver, or their development is controlled by urban capital and institutions, scenery is one natural resource which causes a reverse flow of people out of Vancouver. These landscapes, or scenery, include both the variety of physical features and the character of settlements. New and improved transport has given the urban population of the southwest access to open spaces and to a variety of landscapes which contrast with those of the Lower Mainland. Some of the "unspoiled" rural landscapes of the interior are a counter-attraction to the urban magnet of Greater Vancouver, and provision of recreation and tourist facilities are contributing to the increasing population in the interior.

Certain areas of particular scenic beauty have been set aside as national or provincial parks where certain types of land use are prevented and the areas are maintained for the benefit of visitors. These recreational resources can be classified by function, purpose and area. For example, the National Parks along the British Columbia-Alberta border have spectacular mountain scenery which attracts "consumers" from around the world. Similarly, there is international appeal to the "Inside Passage" along the fiorded coast and protected channels of coastal British Columbia to Alaska. The provincial parks and wilderness areas attract visitors mainly from the urban centres of western North America. The distribution and density of regional recreation and tourist facilities are directly related to the geographical patterns of population distribution in the province. The pressure of "resource-use" is greatest upon the parks, camp sites and picnic areas closest to the high population densities of the southwest coast, or along the Trans-Canada or Okanagan Valley routes.

The recreation or tourist industry is now significant in the total provincial economy, but the value of this scenery-resource cannot be measured simply in dollars. Its social and mental value is likely to become of increasing importance in the leisure time of the 75 percent of the population which is concentrated into the southwestern corner of the province. The distinctive physical environments of coastal climate and the mountain landforms are resources which attract visitors from eastern Canada and are economic assets. Numerous tourists who visit the National Parks in the Rockies continue to the coast in the summer to enjoy the cool, sunny days and the ocean settings. In winter, people with long holidays who wish to stay in Canada, and an increasing number of conventions, come to southwestern British Columbia to escape the severe eastern winters.

goal is to utilize the natural environment and its resources for the provision of jobs and profits. These issues were seldom raised in the days of early European settlement because most people migrated west looking for wealth, and the resource endowment seemed ample for all and for a variety of uses.

Summary

Man's perception and use of the natural environment of British Columbia has certainly changed in the past 100 years. It may be to our economic advantage, and be part of our social policy, to keep the "empty" and unused part of our environment in that state instead of being "developed." The natural endowment of forest, rocks, land and river has been developed by an increasingly ingenious and technically-conscious population. These natural resources have existed in British Columbia since before the explorations of Mackenzie or Vancouver, but the pace of their utilization has now quickened. The human resources, long supplied by immigrants, are now being trained and educated within the region, producing a population which is jealously proud of its resource potential, but beginning to see the environment and its resources differently than the residents of a century ago. Tensions are developing in the province between those dedicated to conservation of a quality environment and those whose main

veral smaller cities vie with one another in supplying goods and services for their regions. Because there are regional differences in economic growth within the province some cities are growing faster than others.

Functional Structure of British Columbia

In the functional structure of British Columbia Vancouver is the primate city. The economy of other provincial regions is organized around a few cities which increasingly act as subregional capitals in a modified hierarchy. The Georgia Strait region is the most important and Vancouver dominates its economy and social life. Its direct hinterland is the Lower Fraser River valley in which few activities are not influenced directly or indirectly by Vancouver. Vancouver's secondary hinterland extends through the Cordillera to the Prairie Provinces for some export commodities. This dominance is undoubtedly related to the flows toward its port, but also is the result of management and financial decisions made in Vancouver. In the interior two cities, Prince George and Kamloops, have effectively established themselves as sub-regional capitals and they are developing their own tributary hinterlands. However, on the North Coast, in the Okanagan Valley and in the Kootenays the dominant cities have not yet emerged and se-

industry, plus improved transport across the Fraser River (bridges and a tunnel), have helped to accelerate the change from rural to urban for many sections on the south side of the river. In addition, new commercial centres have been established in adjacent rapidly growing communities of Burnaby, Coquitlam and Surrey. These centres, including New Westminster, maintain a healthy individuality and serve a sub-regional population of about 200,000 persons. In the multi-nucleii urban system which constitutes Greater Vancouver we are still learning how much New Westminster, Burnaby, Coquitlam and Surrey operate separately as economic and social units, and how much they are inter-connected among themselves and with Vancouver. The satellite suburban cities are certainly part of the functional unit called metropolitan Vancouver but they also maintain a degree of individual identity. Exactly how much integration and separation there is awaits further urban research.

Victoria is focused around its inner harbour, highlighted by the distinctive architecture of the Parliament buildings and the Empress Hotel. The downtown core includes the nearby rehabilitated business and shopping streets. The residential areas of Victoria spread northward rapidly after 1946, and they were followed by spacious suburban shopping plazas, many outside of the political boundaries of the city. About 150,000 persons on Saanich peninsula and nearby southeastern Vancouver Island come at some time to the professional and government services of downtown Victoria. The provincial government, and the federal government at Esquimalt, are the main generators of employment.

To the northward, Nanaimo is the hub of central Vancouver Island. It is about 30 miles across Georgia Strait from Vancouver, and has taken advantage of its intermediate position between the primate city and central and northern Vancouver Island. As coal mining declined and then disappeared from Nanaimo's resource base, it was replaced by transport activities (rail, road and harbour), sawmills and the nearby pulp mill as the main generators of employment. Nanaimo's

Georgia Strait Region

In this region four main urban cores — Vancouver, New Westminster, Victoria, Nanaimo — plus a number of adjoining suburbs and smaller towns, are linked functionally in terms of their industrial, commercial, institutional and recreational operations. Vancouver and Victoria provide certain services for the whole region, but each core performs particular functions for its local area. The hierarchy of urban places is linked in a geographical network which operates as a spatial unit.

New Westminster was the largest town and the "central place" in the Lower Fraser River valley in 1871. The commercial centre of New Westminster, along Columbia Street, became important as a shopping area for people in the rural Fraser Valley, particularly after the river was bridged in 1904. However, this shopping function has declined relative to the increased urbanization of the small towns in the Valley. New growth as a wholesaling and distribution centre for Vancouver Island has probably adversely affected the expansion of commercial activity in Victoria.

Vancouver is a recent city — a product of the twentieth century. It is the chief commercial and industrial city of the region. The tall buildings of its ever-changing downtown skyline hold the major concentration of business, entertainment and retail facilities. It is the main place of work in the Greater Vancouver area, drawing workers and shoppers from relatively high density residential sectors within a radius of about six miles. However, its downtown business core, and nearby industrial zones, are by no means the only major "work places" in the urban complex of Greater Vancouver. (Map No. 11, p. 53)

Like all cities, Vancouver has particular geographical patterns of land uses and urban functions. The various work places are interspersed among large residential areas. The varied terrain with its mountain, ocean and river vistas presented a range of opportunities for expression of individual taste in style and site of housing not as common elsewhere in Canada. Throughout the city a sectoral pattern of residences emerged, segregated mainly on the basis of income and social class. These social and economic differences are apparent in the residential landscapes of the city, particularly in the landscape contrasts between the northeastern and western parts of the city. The wider streets and set-back houses with landscaped front yards of the southwest area are distinct characteristics in the visual urban geography of the city.

By about 1910 the "West End" section, lying between the commercial core and Stanley Park, was occupied by mainly middle and upper income families. Prior to 1940 many low-rise apartments had been built in the West End, but after 1950 it became the main concentration of high-rise apartments in the city, with a high percentage of single persons and young married couples. The West End is now a distinct social region of Vancouver. East of Main Street lower income families built small stucco and frame homes south of the port and industrial area; street after street was filled in with similar houses on narrow lots, set close to the road with small front yards. The East End became the area of "working class" Vancouver — which is not to say that residents elsewhere in the city do not "work".

After 1920 the suburban expansion of single-family detached homes into the former municipalities of Point Grey and South Vancouver was aided and directed by an efficient and low cost electric streetcar service. Industrial workers, professional men or clerical classes alike were able to move away from downtown work places, to purchase land and build homes. The exodus of middle income families to peripheral suburbs was postponed in Vancouver in the late 1930s by the building of the Lions Gate Bridge from Stanley Park to West Vancouver. This bridge permitted a great post-war housing expansion on the North Shore, within a few miles of the downtown core. Long distance commuting to the city core did not accelerate therefore in the 1950s, as was common in other Anglo-American cities at that time. At present, for example, it is estimated that about 90 percent of the people who come to the downtown core daily travel from within a six mile radius. After 1946 a large number of "blue-collar" families and middle income service workers built homes east of Vancouver, in the glacially-deposited uplands of Burnaby, and to the southward on the delta flats of Richmond. Many of these people now work and shop in the peripheral semicircle of business and industry and their trips to the city centre are not frequent. Farther south and east, in Surrey and Coquitlam, these outer residential areas supply low-cost housing sites for people working in the suburban industrial ring which is becoming apparent outside of Vancouver. (Map No. 11, p. 53)

With much of the land within Vancouver itself fully occupied by about 1950, except for an area in the southeast part, the need for multi-family dwellings increased rapidly. In this trend Vancouver is similar to large Eastern Canadian cities. The tall apartment blocks of the West End offered a unique

INDUSTRIAL AREAS OF GREATER VANCOUVER, 1970

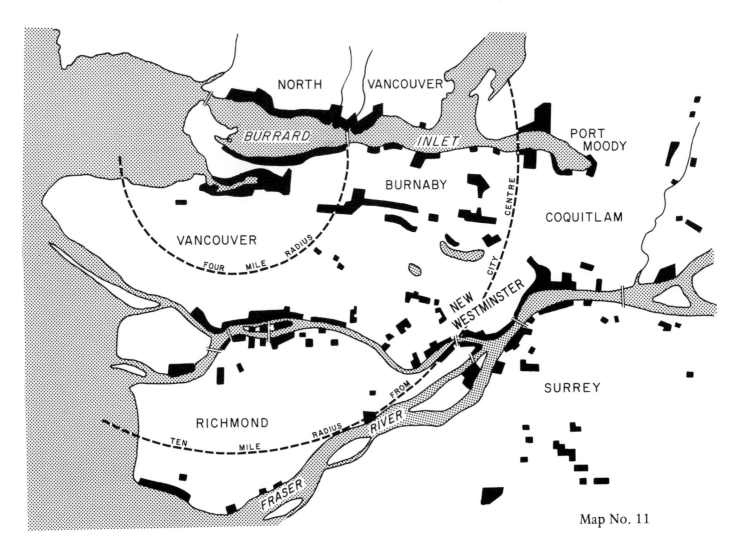

NORTH VANCOUVER

PORT MOODY

BURRARD INLET

BURNABY

COQUITLAM

VANCOUVER

CENTRE

FOUR MILE RADIUS

NEW WESTMINSTER

SURREY

RICHMOND

FROM

TEN MILE RADIUS RIVER

FRASER

Map No. 11

attraction of view and recreational amenities near the down-town core without losing the advantages of proximity. The English Bay apartment skyline is now one of the most impressive in Canada. The West End apartment region has now reached saturation densities, particularly in terms of parking and traffic flow, and as a result of zoning regulations. It is probable that the apartment area of South Granville and Broadway will increase next and expand into old Fairview on the slopes south of False Creek. This trend in changing urban residential patterns is reminiscent of the original areal expansion of single-family residences into the Fairview district after 1890. Another trend in apartment-living is that toward age segregation in housing within the middle and upper-middle class neighbourhoods outside of the core as illustrated by the construction of apartments in the Kerrisdale district of south-western Vancouver and in West Vancouver. Many older persons with grown families are exchanging their family homes in these districts for apartment-living in their old neighbour-hoods.

In Vancouver ethnic differences are less apparent in residential segregation, with a few exceptions, and therefore the distributional geography of these people is not as obvious as other elements in Vancouver's urban landscapes. The area known as "Chinatown" is well-known to tourists. Located south of the old commercial core of Vancouver at the turn of the century, it was first settled by Chinese who had worked in the gold diggings and railway construction in the interior. The visitor to modern Chinatown remembers the attractive restaurants and numerous elderly male Chinese, but seldom sees the young Canadian-born Chinese who are now dispersing their homes throughout the city. The Sikhs, another visual ethnic group, clustered into the area south of False Creek early in this century, near the sawmills where they worked. As the sawmills moved from False Creek so did the nearby concentration of Sikhs dwindle. They moved to the southeast of the city, perhaps to be near the Fraser River sawmills, and they now constitute a notable percentage of the residents near Fraser Ave. and Southeast Marine Drive.

Their turbans and other distinctive clothing which once set them apart have virtually disappeared as the new generation has assimilated into Vancouver's dominant British-origin population. Post-war immigration of Germans, Italians and other Europeans has decreased the former overwhelming British characteristics of Vancouverites. These Europeans have made little impact upon the cultural landscape of the residential areas, but their presence is sometimes apparent in the greater variety of restaurants or in the shopping strips such as "Robsonstrasse" in the West End, "Little Italy" along Commercial Drive or the Greek establishments in Kitsilano. In general, the older parts of the east end of the city are the receiving areas for immigrants; this section now has a greater diversity of central European people than other parts of Vancouver. An analysis of the current distribution of people with distinct national backgrounds awaits the availability of the 1971 census reports.

Although resource-based and industrial payrolls are important throughout British Columbia, one of the major growths in employment has been in the administrative, financial and service occupations. This trend has been particularly noticeable in Vancouver where the percentage of industrial workers and labourers has declined. Vancouver is now a city where the professional and technical, clerical and service, and recreation classes of occupations are dominant. It is estimated that such tertiary-type workers now constitute about 66 percent of the Greater Vancouver labour force. These employment trends, and their related implications in income, housing and other urban conditions, are similar to those known in other large Canadian cities. They should have some impact upon local perceptions of what the future city may be in its urban landscapes. As resource-based economy expanded throughout the province the administration of productive enterprise became more centralized in Vancouver. New pulp mills in Prince George or Prince Rupert, for example, are managed from Vancouver. The range of services which are provided in the interior towns remains small because of the accessibility in Vancouver of firms such as accountants, engineers, insurance, etc.

This concentration of management and finance is a geographical entity apparent in the high-rise office buildings west of Granville Street near the harbour and expanding westward along Georgia and adjoining streets.

The retailing functions of the downtown core have grown rather slowly, but the area has not suffered the absolute decline in business noted in some American cities. Greater numbers in the non-industrial downtown labour force and the increased density of middle and high income residents in apartments close to downtown have helped to maintain retail sales in the core during the time when competing suburban shopping centres were being built. The downtown core has some problems of accessibility. Being on a peninsula means that access from the suburban areas is limited to a few streets and bridges. The proposed provision of new rapid-transit routes and facilities may generate better accessibility for the original core of Vancouver, but it remains to be known whether or not the residents of the satellite cores around the city really need or desire this improved access.

Industrial and wholesale plants are of decreasing significance adjacent to the commercial core of downtown Vancouver. These facilities now form part of a suburban semicircle about six to twelve miles away from the core. (Map No. 11, p. 53) They stretch along the North Arm of the Fraser River where sawmills dominate; they occupy the lowland across central Burnaby served by the Canadian National and Great Northern railways and by major highways. The North Vancouver waterfront is an expanding part of the original industrial strip around the harbour of Vancouver; whereas shipbuilding once dominated in North Vancouver now a wide variety of dockage and industrial enterprises is apparent. About twelve miles out a peripheral ring of industry occupies waterfront sites. Many of these industrial plants manufacture for the Vancouver and British Columbia market, and are successfully competing with imported manufactured goods from Eastern Canada. Along the South Arm of the Fraser River to east of New Westminster there are fish canneries, cement, paper and lumber plants and a variety of other industries. One of the major new facilites is the bulk cargo area at Roberts Bank, a deepwater port built up by dredging off the mouth of the Fraser River. One of its main cargoes is coal for Japan which is moved in unit trains from southeastern B.C. Eastward, other industries are scattered through Coquitlam and occupy the eastern end of Burrard Inlet at Port Moody. The oil refineries there, located on tidewater originally in order to be supplied by California crude oil, are now fed by pipelines from the Interior Plains region. As industrial areas have developed outside of Vancouver these suburban places have become more self-sufficient. Richmond and Surrey, for example, which were becoming "dormitory" suburbs for Greater Vancouver in the 1950s, now have a variety of industries and commerce which supply local employment for their residents.

The numerical growth of the Greater Vancouver area is illustrated by the following table:

Year	Vancouver	New Westminster	North Vancouver	North Shore total	Regional District total
1921	163,000	14,500	7,700	13,500	223,000
1931	247,000	17,500	8,500	20,300	338,000
1941	275,000	23,000	9,000	30,000	395,000
1951	345,000	29,000	16,000	45,000	560,000
1961	385,000	34,000	24,000	90,000	790,000
1971	423,000	42,000	32,000	125,000	1,026,000

In summary, the Georgia Strait region is an urban-industrial area dominated by downtown Vancouver. The region is integrated functionally in many ways even though the component parts, such as Victoria and Nanaimo, are not contiguous to the urbanized area of Vancouver. This physical separation of the functional region is partly the result of the particular distribution of land and water and partly a reflection of settlement history. As time-distance shrinks the Georgia Strait region is becoming a more closely integrated regional unit.

Sub-Regional Capitals

The regional centres in the interior are in the 15,000 to 40,000 population range. (Map No. 12, p. 57) Unlike in Ontario where this size of city competes poorly with larger cities nearby, several of the interior cities of British Columbia are growing rapidly into sub-regional capitals. Although remnants of their early establishment can still be seen, their buildings have a fresh, new physical appearance, because most construction has taken place in the past two decades. In general, the commercial cores are about three or four blocks in area, and as the population passes about 10,000 persons, suburban shopping centres have been established. Differentiation in the residential zones is being created as the view areas and upper slopes near the old towns are being occupied by better housing.

Prince George, the major city of the central interior, has grown rapidly in the past decade. Its central significance in the interior forestry industry has previously been discussed; its pulp mills and sawmills, and secondary supply and construction industries, give it a strong resource base. In addition, Prince George also performs other urban functions for the northern interior region. The commercial core of downtown Prince George expanded outward as it became the main supply and service centre for central British Columbia. As in Vancouver at the turn of the century, the original houses near the old commercial core of Prince George were torn down and replaced by modern stores and offices. Some of the once-numerous sawmills along the railway near the commercial core have been replaced by warehouse and wholesale buildings — similar to the geographical pattern of sawmill migration from the edges of the Vancouver downtown core 30 or 40 years ago. The commercial and service sphere of influence of Prince George reaches south to Quesnel, west beyond Burns Lake and northeast through the Rocky Mountain Trench to the Peace River area. The new railway links to the northwest are bringing the resources of Stuart and Takla lakes into the Prince George hinterland. As the largest city in the central interior Prince George has about reached the population threshold where it can generate some of its own internal service industries and occupations. One should keep a scale on Prince George's population increases, however, in comparison with the numerical increase in metropolitan Vancouver. The population increase of 8,000 persons in Prince George in 1966-71 is only one-third of the 24,000 persons added to the population of Delta in this same period.

Kamloops occupies a strategic transportation position where the North and South Thompson rivers join. From along these valleys the Canadian National and Canadian Pacific railways converged and the Trans-Canada and Yellowhead highways joined. Many occupations are therefore dependent on the railcars and automobiles which stop in Kamloops for servicing or to pick up or deposit cargoes. As the main "central place" in the Thompson Valley region, Kamloops supplies goods and services to the ranching, forestry and mining economies of the south-central interior. It also has an important

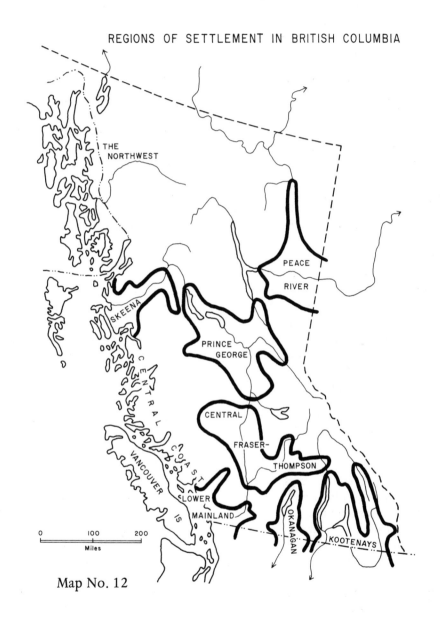

REGIONS OF SETTLEMENT IN BRITISH COLUMBIA

THE NORTHWEST

PEACE RIVER

SKEENA

CENTRAL COAST

PRINCE GEORGE

CENTRAL

FRASER-THOMPSON

VANCOUVER IS.

LOWER MAINLAND

OKANAGAN

KOOTENAYS

0   100   200
Miles

Map No. 12

57

government function, having been chosen as the site of many regional offices of the provincial government. Like Prince George, its industrial base is mainly the forestry industry but this is not the sole base of its economy. As Prince George and Kamloops grow areally and numerically, and increase their urban functions, one might recall that the significance of their geographical positions was apparent even 150 years ago when the fur-trading posts were founded.

In the Okanagan Valley the economic rivalry between the three main cities is intense and no single centre yet dominates the Valley. The concept of central place and the centralization of service functions would suggest that Kelowna may gain the largest share of the regional economy, especially those functions related to government. Kelowna also has the largest area of adjoining agricultural land in its direct hinterland. Penticton became the closest Okanagan city to Vancouver when the Hope-Princeton highway was opened after World War II, and its beaches became an accessible tourist attraction. The lines of motels in Penticton are visual reminders of the importance of tourists in the local economy during the summer. Vernon lagged behind the other cities during the 1950s, but the opening of the Trans-Canada Highway brought it close to Calgary and its holiday trade. If these new transportation links were important to the regional economy of the three Okanagan cities, then perhaps the new highway link through Richter Pass to Osoyoos may change the economy of the southern end of the Okanagan Valley.

Behind the tourist and recreation functions of the Valley cities lies the basic manufacturing economy of fruit processing. Each city has about equal amounts of this industrial base. The disadvantage of smaller areas of available irrigated land in the southern Okanagan is balanced by the advantages of better climate in the south. Since expanded markets for fruit seem less than favourable, industrial growth based on fruit processing in the Okanagan cities is not likely — and if other industrial growth is at the expense of its attractive physical environment it may not be desirable to local residents.

In the West Kootenay region there are also three cities, Trail, Castlegar and Nelson competing for dominance. The areal expansion of each will be limited by the small amount of level land near their valley sites. Trail, and its dormitory-city, Rossland, houses the large number of industrial workers and management personnel of the huge smelter-refinery-fertilizer plant. Its industrial base is strong, but its service functions are less developed. Nelson has been by-passed by the building of a highway between Salmo and Creston and may lose some of its transport functions. Castlegar has central location in the Valley; it is near the Arrow Lake dam and pulp mill, and has a regional college. Actually Trail, East Trail, Kinnaird and Castlegar are almost one long, dispersed city in the Columbia River valley. With better north-south transport the functions of the various urban centres could begin to supplement one another and a new type of topographically-controlled linear city may emerge.

In the East Kootenay region, Cranbrook is increasing more rapidly in population than is Kimberley, but they are close enough together to supply supplementary industrial and commercial functions. This southern Rocky Mountain Trench area was rather dormant after 1950, compared with the resource development of other regions of interior British Columbia, but a new pulp mill, increased sawmilling and the employment activity related to coal mining in the Crowsnest Pass is reviving urban growth. If sub-regional integration of the economy ultimately takes place in the East Kootenays, Cranbrook has the geographical position to grow as the largest city.

In the northwest, near the western end of the Skeena Valley, Prince Rupert, Terrace and Kitimat are separate urban entities. Prince Rupert has the advantage of early origin, established facilities and links to Alaska. It is the terminal of the northern highway as well as the northern railway. The promise of improved harbour facilities and increased resource development in its direct hinterland may yet permit Prince Rupert to capitalize on its "northern outlet" position. How-

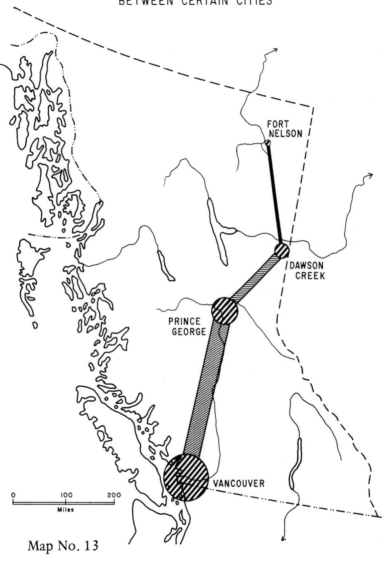

SCHEMATIC DIAGRAM OF HIERARCHY OF LINKAGE AND FUNCTIONS
BETWEEN CERTAIN CITIES

FORT
NELSON

DAWSON
CREEK

PRINCE
GEORGE

VANCOUVER

0   100   200
Miles

Map No. 13

ever, the central city of the group, Terrace, may tap the formerly dormant resources of the Bulkley Valley east of it and supply services to that hinterland rather than from Prince Rupert. Terrace and Kitimat are close enough to share some of their service and commercial functions. Terrace controls the entrance to a topographic gateway to the north where the Nass Valley leads beyond to Stewart and the northwestern interior. In the emerging geographical network of cities, services, hinterlands and transport evolving in northern British Columbia it will be interesting to see if the resources and activities of the area east of Panhandle Alaska will be attracted to Terrace and Prince Rupert by roads or will be pulled by the new railway to Prince George.

In the northeast changes have become apparent in the relative importance of segments of the regional economy of the Peace River area. Two cities, Dawson Creek and Fort St. John, compete for the position of regional capital of this area. When the region was only agricultural Dawson Creek was the only sizeable service centre; it was the end of rail from Alberta and in the centre of the largest area of cleared land, which was then south of the Peace River. From a population of 3,600 in 1951 Dawson Creek increased to 11,000 in 1961, but had only a small increase in the past decade to 12,000 persons. When the Peace River was bridged for the Alaska Highway during World War II and post-war exploration and development of petroleum and natural gas took place north of the river, Fort St. John became a supply and service centre. From a village of 900 persons in 1951 the city expanded to 8,300 population in 1971. The extension of the British Columbia Railway to Fort Nelson in 1971 brought the far northeast into the hinterland of Fort St. John. The links of the northeast region, like those in the East Kootenays of the southeast, are still split between Alberta and the southwestern core of British Columbia. But the commercial and service dominance of Edmonton over the economy of northwestern Canada is being challenged by Prince George. Fort Nelson, for example, is now probably the end of a geographical network and hierarchy of urban centres of increasing size

from Fort St. John, to Dawson Creek, to Prince George to Vancouver. (Map No. 13, p. 59)

Conclusion

Throughout the past 100 years the character of the economy of British Columbia has been greatly influenced by changing concepts of two main factors: its geographical situation, with its actual and relative isolation; and the use of its particular mixture of natural resources or raw materials. Isolation has always been a factor in the social life and economy of people of the province. Throughout the brief period of European settlement most of the people have clustered into the southwestern corner. Those who spread themselves thinly along the interior valleys 50 to 100 years ago well knew the problem of isolation and the resulting high cost of obtaining and maintaining transportation. Just as the Georgia Strait core region was separated from the rest of the world so were the interior and northern settlements cut off from government, head offices and supply firms in the southwest. The psychological and economic effects of isolation, both as a result of the landform character of the region and of its geographical position in the world, have influenced its geographical patterns as well as the outlook of its people.

Peripheral west coast location has always affected British Columbia's development. It delayed exploration and settlement; it made it difficult for the reserves of natural resources to enter world markets; it probably colours the views of the people on national and world affairs. British Columbians were mainly coastal dwellers throughout much of their modern history and many of them look to the Pacific. They shared this ocean orientation with peoples in California and the nearby Northwest states; with these American people they developed strong north-south connections. The Canadian and American west coast areas have much in common, and they differ in many ways from the eastern parts of the continent. Being far away from the old industrial and populated heartlands of eastern Anglo-America, the west coast region developed different links and connections within this continent and with the rest of the world. These links resulted in a variety of ideas and technology being received from many different parts of the world. Settlers reached the west coast late in comparison with the other areas of present dense settlement in Anglo-America. The region was far from Britain by sea and far from the Canadian eastern heartland by land. Few of the many people who flowed out of western Europe and the British Isles in the 19th century reached British Columbia. After they came the physical separation by distance, mountains and ocean was real.

For much of the past 100 years native-born British Columbians were a minority; the adults in business, industry or government were those to whom "home" was somewhere else. After about 1920 more and more of the provincial population was derived from Canadians who had spent several years on the Prairies or in Eastern Canada. This steady westward migration of Canadians became a major flow after 1945. As new generations were born in the region, however, they became aware of how their lives were influenced by such external matters as eastern manufacturers, freight rates, economic conditions in northwestern Europe, and "neglect" by the federal government in the East. However, the people who came to British Columbia were little different in national or ethnic background from those who immigrated to Ontario, except for the sprinkling of South and East Asians. It is likely that the climate and scenic landscapes of Vancouver were significant attractions; the region probably also attracted those with aggressive enthusiasm who were hoping to utilize the resource endowment in a new type of Canadian "pioneering". This mixture of "easterners" with the increasing native-born population loosened the cultural isolation and created more personal ties with Eastern Canada.

The heritage and influence of large numbers of farmers, who have been part of Eastern Canada's population, have never been significant in British Columbia. The "rural life" which older people in Ontario cities remember in inaccurate detail is not part of the culture of native-born British Columbians. With only one large local urban market, with a limited amount of level land, and having the counter-attraction of other resources with external markets, agriculture never became of wide-spread importance. The provincial population has been, and is, urban — whether the "urban" meant a mining town, a logging camp or a fish cannery early in the century, or one of the many occupations of present-day economic life in the Georgia Strait region.

In the past, without a large local consuming market, the development and utilization of the raw materials from the forest, sea and rocks of the region were usually determined by markets, transportation and capital investment supplied from external places. Industry relied upon producing for this export market and secondary manufacturing developed only slowly. When secondary industries were established in recent decades they were often branch plants opened by eastern manufacturers. Management decisions could be made on the basis of their national policy rather than on regional needs. The complaints and resentment which some Canadians have expressed over American investment and branch plants,

despite their need and value to Canadian economy, were repeated in the "economic colonialism" which was felt by some British Columbians with regard to Ontario. As local markets increased in size in British Columbia and local companies were formed and prospered one can now hear these same complaints from residents of interior British Columbia about the dominance of Vancouver!

British Columbia is undoubtedly dominated by metropolitan Vancouver. Not only does the urban region have half of the population of British Columbia, it has much of the management and financial control of the resource development of the province. It seems unlikely that this dominance of Vancouver is detrimental to the growth and future economic prosperity of the rest of the province. Even though the interior settlements are growing rapidly in population, they are still small by Ontario or Quebec comparisons; and their growth in actual numbers is small compared with the annual increase in population in Greater Vancouver.

British Columbia is a distinctive part of Canada. Many of its characteristics and contrasts are becoming increasingly apparent, but in other ways the regional economy and landscapes are similar to features in other parts of Canada. The spectacular landforms, the unique coastal climate and the large coniferous trees are obvious physical characteristics which are not found in similar combinations elsewhere in Canada. The towns and cities of British Columbia usually have attractive physical sites, but in general the form and structures of these urban places differ very little from similar-sized cities elsewhere in Canada.

Functional unity within British Columbia is well established and is being strengthened. One hundred years ago the southwestern corner was the most significant area in the western Cordillera of Canada. Now the coast and interior operate together and the whole region is more closely interconnected with the economy of Canada and of the world. Throughout the century some geographical patterns have changed very little; others have kept the same form but increased their densities; in other cases new geographical patterns have emerged. Just as political, social and economic changes can be traced through the past century, so can one map and discuss the geographical changes.

Cover photograph: The Vancouver Public Library

This book has been published with the help of a grant from the
Social Science Research Council of Canada, using funds provided
by the Canada Council.